Journeying toward Renewal

a spiritual companion for pastoral sabbaticals

Melissa Bane Sevier

Foreword by William F. Brosend II

An Alban Institute Publication

Library of Congress Catalog Card Number 2002109036

ISBN 1-56699-273-7

Contents

The picture is memorable—a path leading into the cool green growth beneath a towering forest. The words are inviting and hopeful—*granting pastors a time apart*. The picture and words have also been effective—in recent years pastoral leaders have made thousands of inquiries to the Louisville Institute in response to this advertisement, resulting in scores of sabbatical grants. Untold additional inquiries yielded hundreds of grants through the state and national clergy renewal programs of the Louisville Institute's parent organization, Lilly Endowment Inc. One of their grantees was the author of this book, Melissa Bane Sevier.

A time apart. I do not know a single pastor or pastoral leader whose heart does not in some measure thrill at the possibilities the phrase invokes. Not just to get away *from*—though Lord knows there is a good bit of that—but to get away *for* and *to*. Because finally sabbatical, like sabbath, is not about avoidance and escape but encounter and embrace. Yes, the idea of a few months without board, session, vestry, council or committee meetings has its appeal. After a while, though, one learns that when you've missed one meeting, you've missed them all, and the crucial question is what one does with the time gained from all the meetings you've missed. Any pastor who thinks nothing will happen while she or he is away may not have adequate experience to merit a sabbatical. Melissa Sevier missed a lot. Her sabbatical took place in the late summer and fall of 2001. September 11th fell one month into her leave.

Other preachers who found themselves without a pulpit that week can well imagine her relief and regret at not presiding over an evening prayer service on Tuesday or Wednesday, and not offering a sermon that Sunday. Any pastoral leader wondering how to handle absence in the times of crisis that probably will occur during a sabbatical leave will learn much from Melissa's experience. Yet this is hardly the only part of her experience from which we may learn. One of the privileges of reading *Journeying toward Renewal* is that the author invites us to share in more than one side of her life and ministry.

We first meet the Reverend Sevier as she recognizes, some eight years into her service as pastor of the First Presbyterian Church of Aurora, Indiana, that she may well have waited longer than she should have to take her first sabbatical. In a phrase that will resonate with many, she describes herself not as "burnt out," but as "in a rut of stagnant leadership." She allows us to follow her through the self-doubts and delays that precede her decision to seek a sabbatical, and the missteps that inevitably come before finding her own path and plan. In each chapter Sevier helpfully interweaves relevant studies, statistics, and conversations with her own experience and reflections, and offers thoughts for inspiration, for contemplation, and for action, along with suggested readings. We learn about planning and adjusting a sabbatical, taking leave from the congregation and taking the sabbatical, returning to the congregation, and evaluating the sabbatical. It is rich learning.

The last few years have brought tremendous change to the landscape of pastoral sabbaticals, due in no small measure (modesty aside) to the initiatives of the Louisville Institute and Lilly Endowment Inc. This change has come through advertising and advocacy, through the hundreds of sabbatical and clergy renewal grants to pastoral leaders and churches, and most importantly, through the changes these sabbaticals fostered and nurtured in the pastoral leaders themselves. There has been, then, a significant increase in the number of pastoral leaders who are able to experience a meaningful time of sabbatical renewal. There has also been a certain "institutionalizing" of pastoral sabbaticals— what was once rare has not only become more common, it has become institutionalized, included in the call packages recommended by the judicatories of many denominations, expected and requested by pastors who negotiate their own compensation.

What there has not been as yet is what one might call a *deepening* of pastoral sabbaticals, and a body of experience with sabbaticals from which others may draw. *Journeying toward Renewal* is a significant contribution to this deepening. While we await more systematic study of the pastoral sabbatical experience, Melissa Sevier's book offers an in-depth reflection on one pastor's time apart.

Almost all of the applicants to the Louisville Institute's *Sabbatical Grants for Pastoral Leaders* program are planning their first sabbatical, usually to their own and their congregation's amazement. While sabbatical is surely something one does better the second time around, like most pastoral leaders I feel fortunate to have had one. *Journeying toward Renewal* will be a valuable resource for pastoral leaders and their parishioners who may have a hard time imagining what a sabbatical will look and feel like. For the time being, reading Melissa Sevier may be as close as we can come to having an *experience* of sabbatical before we have the sabbatical itself.

WILLIAM F. BROSEND II
The Louisville Institute

Acknowledgments

I am grateful to so many for their contributions to my sabbatical and to this book. Editor David Lott at the Alban Institute has encouraged and nurtured the entire project, giving life to what was formerly just an idea. Without his support, the book would not have happened.

My sabbatical was made possible by a clergy renewal grant from Lilly Endowment Inc. Though I am sure I would have made the sabbatical happen some other way without a grant, the gift certainly made it easier on me and the congregation. Jean M. Smith, program director in the religion division, has also been extremely helpful in the research of the book.

The life of this book comes from the experiences and expertise of the clergy and judicatory officials I have interviewed. I am grateful to each one of them for their time and thoughtful responses to all my questions:

- Ellen Acton, pastor of Southfield Presbyterian Church, PC(USA), Southfield, Michigan;
- Jim Antal, pastor of Plymouth Church (UCC), Shaker Heights, Ohio;
- Mark Asman, rector of Trinity Episcopal Church, Santa Barbara, California;
- Brent Bill, associate director, the Indianapolis Center for Congregations;

- Arthur Boers, assistant professor of pastoral theology, Associated Mennonite Biblical Seminary, and former pastor of Bloomingdale Mennonite Church, Bloomingdale, Ontario;
- William F. Brosend II, associate director, the Louisville Institute;
- Michael Cohen, executive director, North American offices, Arava Institute for Environmental Studies, and Rabbi Emeritus, Israel Congregation, Manchester Center, Vermont;
- Cheryl Ann Elfond, general presbyter, Transylvania Presbytery, PC(USA);
- Richard Herman, vice president, Wheat Ridge Ministries, Itasca, Illinois;
- David Holte, pastor of Trinity Lutheran Church, Brainerd, Minnesota;
- Jeff Hosmer, pastor of Northminster Presbyterian Church, PC(USA), Cincinnati, Ohio;
- Jill Hudson, executive presbyter, Presbytery of Whitewater Valley, PC(USA);
- Arland Jacobson, executive director of the CHARIS Ecumenical Center, Concordia College, Moorhead, Minnesota;
- Linda C. Johnson, associate rector, Trinity Episcopal Church, Bloomington, Indiana, and chaplain to Indiana University;
- Carol McDonald, co-executive, Synod of Lincoln Trails, PC(USA);
- Holly McKissick, pastor of St. Andrew Christian Church (Disciples), Olathe, Kansas;
- Michael Mather, pastor of Broadway Christian Parish (UMC), South Bend, Indiana;
- Steven Carr Reuben, rabbi of Kehillat Israel Reconstructionist Synagogue, Pacific Palisades, California;
- Sam Roberson, executive presbyter, Cincinnati Presbytery, PC(USA);

- Peter Rogness, bishop, St. Paul Area Synod, Evangelical Lutheran Church in America (ELCA);
- Bill Schooler, pastor of Saint Jude Catholic Church, Fort Wayne, Indiana;
- Harris Schultz, interim pastor of Sycamore Presbyterian Church, PC(USA), Cincinnati, Ohio;
- Thom M. Shuman, pastor of Greenhills Community Presbyterian Church, PC(USA), Cincinnati, Ohio.

In addition, Richard J. Bruesehoff, director of leadership support for the Evangelical Church in America and co-author of another Alban Institute book about sabbaticals, *Clergy Renewal*, has been tremendously helpful in pointing me to the right resources and supporting the concept of this volume.

My friends and fellow journeyers in this sabbatical are the members at First Presbyterian Church in Aurora, Indiana. The church's session urged me to go forward with the sabbatical plan and supported me all the way through. Never once did anyone complain about my being gone for 15 weeks, yet they all welcomed me with open arms when I returned. They also took a sabbatical from me and our regular way of doing things, and hired the Reverend Florence Beaujon to preach and carry out pastoral duties in my absence. Florence remains close to our hearts because of her devotion, and as the person who was present with the congregation during and after the tragedies of September 11, 2001. In addition, Carol Lempke, church secretary, kept all things running smoothly and took on new tasks while I was gone.

I am also grateful to the members of West Cincinnati Presbyterian Church and to their pastor, Richard McNeill. They welcomed me warmly as I worshiped with them during my sabbatical and they offered me a home away from my home church.

Finally, and most importantly, my husband Jerry is always my biggest supporter. He is the one who keeps me stable and who made my sabbatical experience all the richer because we shared it.

In the autumn of 2001 I was privileged to take a sabbatical, after working in the same congregation for nine-and-a-half years. Today I continue working happily in that congregation, a situation that might have been much less satisfactory for all parties without my time away. I might even have considered leaving.

Before and during the sabbatical, I kept a journal as spiritual practice, a discipline I have kept off and on for many years. Even now, the journal helps me see the course I have taken from stress to health, to renewal, to recommitment in my parish setting. Without moving to a new place, I have nevertheless traveled a journey of faith and newness.

In the course of my own musings, I grew curious about the experiences of others who had taken sabbaticals, and began to seek them out. I learned that though we all approached sabbatical differently and had varied results, to a person we found the experience spiritually renewing. It was then I decided to write a book that would be a spiritual companion to those considering or taking sabbaticals. In addition, the book offers serious and practical advice for the sabbatical journey, from the beginning of the idea to the final result.

As I speak to pastors and others about the subject of this book, I hear a growing interest in the concept of clergy sabbaticals. That probably shouldn't be a surprise, since pastors and congregations alike are looking for spiritual renewal and are often hoping to continue their relationship together for many years without growing stale.

On the other hand, this book is not just for pastors who are in the midst of sabbatical. If you are thinking about renewal leave, or if you sense a need for rejuvenation in your spiritual or work life, I hope this book will give you ideas and inspiration for pursuing your dreams. If, though, you are currently preparing for or are in the middle of your sabbatical, the book may serve as a spiritual companion for your experience.

I hope you will find this book as I intend it: a reflection on and support for the continuation of our spiritual journeys as we move into new territory, then return home renewed and refreshed.

Chapter 1

The Right Time?

Journal: How I Came to Know I Needed a Sabbatical

Spring 2000 (Friday Morning)

It has been another of those weeks. Every pastor, I imagine, has them. It started with a lousy sermon (mine) on Sunday and went downhill from there. Today is my supposed day off, and I will be spending most of today and tomorrow catching up on things that did not get done this week. Worse, on my desk is another lousy sermon waiting to be preached in two days. I have looked at it at least five times and cannot figure how to fix it. It is bad when the preacher is bored by and sick of her own sermon.

In between these two bad sermons I have conducted a funeral, with all the pastoral care that entails, and have visited several people several times in the hospital and others at home. I taught a class of youth and spoke with someone about joining the church. I counseled a couple that wants to be married and another couple that wants to stay married and two individuals in personal crisis. I fielded complaints about things over which I have no control and resolved a dispute over an issue so minor I have to strain two days later to remember what it was about. I listened to members give equal expressions of delight and disgust over a new hymn. I began planning Vacation Bible School and devotions for a week of summer camp. I hosted a Seder, participated in choir practice, and attended a Lenten dinner for the women of the community. I wrote a new sermon for three weeks from now and planned that service, and I worked with the secretary on the worship bulletin for this week.

It was not really such an unusual or tough-sounding week, but I have put in a lot of hours, I am tired, and I am not yet finished.

I am so completely exhausted by working seven days a week that I can hardly think about starting over again each Monday morning. Sometimes I simply have to make the time to do things for me: spend time with my husband; garden; cook; read for fun instead of for work. I rarely have time for the reflection that would make me a better pastor.

There are some good things, of course. All is not bleak. We have more young families and children attending and joining the church than in recent memory. Worship attendance is up. Our music program is fantastic. We continue in our mission giving and work. I remain enthusiastic. I love the people and the church, but I am worn out. And, at home, Jerry is as supportive as always. The things I love to do with him or alone are waiting for me, if I can come up with the time and energy.

The worst part of whatever is going on in me must be most evident to others in my sermons, but I see it in all my work. It is a lack of creativity. I feel as though I am "going through the motions" of preaching, teaching, leading worship, and handling pastoral care, administration, and committee work. The goal is visible, but I have to run through foot-deep molasses to reach it.

When I look back over the general notes I have kept over the past eight years since we arrived here, I think I can say objectively that the church and I have accomplished much together. In terms of mission, worship, education, improvements on the building, gaining new members, and finances, we have made some important strides.

When I try to look ahead, however, I see myself in a rut of stagnant leadership. Same old same old, season after season, year after year. There may be enough in the church to keep me interested, but not enough in me that is interesting. I am the one who has stagnated, not the church. The quality of my work is suffering from the number of hours I put in, and I am not sure what to do about that. I am usually energized by the variety of things my job allows me to do, but as of late I am enervated by the workload.

Is it time for me to look for another church? Perhaps a new setting would rejuvenate me. Perhaps a new pastor would be better for the church.

The Need for Clergy Renewal

It would be nearly a year and a half after writing the above journal entry before I would take my clergy renewal leave—my sabbatical. Looking back, though, at my journal from that time period, it is obvious I needed help and renewal in a serious way. As pastor of a 150-member church that averages about 80 for Sunday worship, I am typical of many: We work long hours for many years without relief. Like people in many other professions in our day, we have difficulty drawing appropriate boundaries between our work and our personal lives. Often, the personal life gets swallowed up gradually into the work life until they are no longer distinguishable. Our families suffer, we suffer, our churches suffer.

Maybe it is that last item which has not been examined often enough. Our churches suffer because they lose their formerly rested, energetic pastor to one who is overwhelmed by responsibilities that begin to feel more like chores than like fulfilling a vocation.

Congregational consultant Roy Oswald, in his book *Clergy Self-Care*,[1] discusses the problems with the work lives of many clergy. Determined to answer God's call in a particular church, seeing the neverending needs and unlimited possibilities of that church, hoping to bring out the best in its members, they find themselves unable to do all they wish to do. Instead of setting realistic expectations, they often believe that by their own effort they can make things happen—if they just work a little harder, do a little more, make a few extra phone calls, attend another meeting. And on it goes.

Perhaps the idea of *call* to a church vocation makes the job of a pastor more difficult to put aside at the end of the day than some other jobs. If this is truly my calling, shouldn't I be willing to take it home with me and live it 24/7? How can I not make those visits on the way home? How can I refuse any request?

My husband Jerry is a sales manager for a large company, and we believe he is every bit as called to his work as I am to mine. There seems to be a difference, though, in the expectations our different calls elicit. When he makes a presentation, he does not do it in front of a room of people who issued him a "call" to his position. His sales calls may represent the company, but not in the same way that my pastoral calls represent a local manifestation of the people of God. If he were to discuss his sense of call to his work with most of his colleagues, he would be met mostly with blank stares and people trying to change the subject. My call is something that is understood at every committee meeting. And "call" in church work carries with it the connotation of service, even sacrificial service after the example of Jesus. It is hard for me to form boundaries around that type of service when I am attempting to be balanced.

Ideally, every member of the church sees her work as a calling. However, the entire church believes beyond a doubt that the pastor's work is a calling. Does the sense of vocation include in it the idea that the pastor's life be subsumed under the overarching needs of the church? Of course not, but that is what often occurs.

I am not convinced that pastors work harder than people in other jobs, but I do believe their own expectations and the expectations of the people they work for and with may be quite different from what many other professions experience.

So many pastors are afraid to say they are weary, overwhelmed, or frustrated by their work. They might sound like whiners. They fear the implications of their own questions: Are they questioning their very call to that particular church, or even to the ministry at all? It looks better for everyone if they can just suck it up and keep on going.

Obviously, as Oswald points out so well, sucking it up leads to all sorts of problems, from illness to burnout to leaving the church or the ministry. Then the fears of facing the problem head-on turn into self-fulfilling prophecy. No one, least of all the church, is well served by a pastor who is sick or burned out or gone.

In my case, long before my sabbatical time finally arrived, I did become sick. I had several stress-related illnesses and went to a therapist on the suggestion of my physician to learn stress reduction techniques. Those techniques helped a great deal, but they did not completely solve the problem. The problem was overwork, and for me it took a sabbatical to get out from under what had become the normal way of doing things so I could adopt a healthier work style.

In the meantime, I was able to gain enough control over my situation and my reaction to it to function quite well. I highly recommend that anyone with job-related stress get help from whatever source necessary to live with the immediate and long-term stresses. When I got well, I realized how much I wanted to keep from falling under the control of those stresses again.

Sabbath was what I needed—a way of stepping back and looking at my work in a new and fresh way. I wanted to stay in that church, but I had to change some things about my work. I needed spiritual and creative renewal.

I am definitely not alone. Statistics show stress is a problem many clergy face, and perhaps is simply a part of the ministerial landscape. My denomination, the Presbyterian Church (USA), conducted a survey in 1996 and found not unsurprising results in the area of clergy stress:

Stress on the Job

It's the affliction of the 1990s, and Presbyterian ministers are not exempt:

- 12% of pastors, 15% of specialized clergy experience stress at work *almost every day*
- 18% of pastors, 17% of specialized clergy experience work stress *several days a week*
- 40% of pastors, 38% of specialized clergy experience work stress *once or twice a week.*

In short, large majorities of Presbyterian clergy—whether in the parish or not—experience job-related stress at least weekly, and around one in seven do so on a daily or near-daily basis.

Specific factors contributing to their stress, in order of importance for pastors (as a group, although not necessarily for any one minister) are:

- burnout, overwork, and unrealistic demands from others;
- problems with the session and/or congregation;
- lack of fit between their personalities and work demands; and
- sexual harassment.[2]

Pastoral theologian Arthur Boers, formerly a Mennonite pastor in Canada, left one church "depleted and tired," and knew he did not want to repeat that in the next congregation, so he negotiated a sabbatical in his next contract.

In my case, I am not sure I would ever have been able to renegotiate my "contract" with myself and the church about overwork without significant time away. I wanted to stay in the same place and had no desire to move. Sabbatical leave would provide that option for me. Afterwards, I returned a different and better pastor.

According to Pastor Glenn Ludwig, author of *In It for the Long Haul*, a book that celebrates and supports long-term pastorates "... there are times when our calls must be reissued, if you will; times when we will need to reassess our call to serve in a particular setting to discover what God has in mind for us and for those who called us."[3] Many pastors and congregations would like to stay together for more than the typical few years, and need to find a way to do so that is healthy and strong. A sabbatical can provide the time and space to reassess the call to a renewed life in the same place.

Brent Bill, associate director of the Indianapolis Center for Congregations, quotes a recent study by the Alban Institute, *The Leadership Situation Facing American Congregations: An Alban Institute Special Report*, which says that American clergy and congregations are "caught in a sea change of turmoil and ferment, crisis and opportunity."[4] Bill says:

> The turmoil and crisis shows itself in things such as a shortage of clergy across the American religious landscape, a lowering of the quality of pastoral leadership, the lack of retention of women in clergy ministry, and [the fact] that 40 percent of clergy report that they are facing burnout or severe burnout. These all demonstrate the need for taking a serious look at pastoral sabbaticals. Our work with congregations shows that well-planned sabbaticals strengthen both pastors and congregations [by] giving pastors an opportunity for renewal through

intentional study, rest and reflection as they step away, for a brief period, from the daily demands of congregational life. Pastors return from their sabbaticals with a renewed sense of pastoral purpose and reenergization for the work they feel called to do. That in turn renews and reenergizes the congregation. It's a win-win situation for both parties.

Congregations need stable leaders who model the balanced life.

There are times when a pastor should definitely *not* take a sabbatical. For instance, had I not learned to control my reaction to the stresses in my work, it would have been a mistake to use a sabbatical for that purpose. What I needed early on was counseling, not sabbatical. Only after I had become healthier did I think a sabbatical could be valuable in helping me continue my long-term pastorate, relearning and building on those healthy patterns of ministry.

Lilly Endowment Inc., a granting institution for clergy sabbaticals, takes care to ensure that the pastors who are accepted for grants are ready for self-directed study programs and not in need of serious intervention for burnout or major stress. The Endowment desires to support churches and their pastors by fostering wellness, thereby encouraging pastors in their vocation.

A sabbatical is not for clergy who are burned out; however, it may keep us from becoming burned out by giving us renewal in spirit, vision, and call.

Pastors also should not consider a sabbatical if there are serious family or personal problems or if there is a significant church conflict. These situations require immediate and strong intervention, but a sabbatical is not the right remedy.

Judicatory executive Carol McDonald adds that a pastor shouldn't engage in clergy leave if the congregation is in the midst of making a serious decision—for example, about a building project, a capital campaign, or about making a public witness statement.

Finally, a sabbatical is not for the purpose of deciding if it is time for you to change churches, or to let the church get used to not having you around because you have already decided to change churches. It is unfair to the congregation to ask them to give you a renewal leave when that's what you plan to do: *leave*. It is also unfair to subsequent pastors because the church will be less likely to put themselves in that situation again. A sabbatical is for renewal in the place where God has put you.

An interesting observation arose from my interviews with pastors who have taken sabbaticals. Among those whose churches had a sabbatical policy, and who took the sabbatical policy on schedule, there appeared to be a more balanced view about the clergy leave time. Sabbatical was a normal expectation between pastor and congregation, and pastors were able to anticipate the program with pleasure and excitement, instead of desperate need.

Jim Antal, an Ohio pastor, had such a policy with his congregation. The congregation knew when it called him that he would take three months of leave after five years of service. Expectations were clear up front. He was able to look forward to the sabbatical rather than wait until it was "needed." Nevertheless, when five years had elapsed, he was well aware that a pastor of a nearby congregation had often been criticized for always being away. Jim decided to take his three months in one-month increments to reduce the opportunity for criticism. It worked well for him, he said, because he is able to switch back and forth easily between the two worlds of parish work and sabbatical leave. Others might not find it so simple.

Some aspects of sabbatical are not simple for many. Though statistics are not available, anecdotally it appears that clergywomen are far less likely to take sabbaticals than their male counterparts. When I asked clergywomen why they thought this might be the case, I received several answers. Many women serve smaller churches where resources are less available. Others serve as associate or assistant pastors in churches where it's only acceptable for the senior pastor to take a sabbatical. Women who are co-pastors with their husbands find it extremely difficult to negotiate simultaneous sabbatical time for both of them and are left with the choice of taking turns. Many women serve in specialized ministry where sabbaticals often are not an option: as chaplains, educators, and so forth. It may be true that women are less socialized to negotiate for what they want and need, such as salary increases and renewal leave time. The most often mentioned difficulty for women clergy taking sabbaticals was that of family needs, especially regarding children or elderly parents. Whatever the reasons, clergywomen should be encouraged to seek renewal for their pastoral ministry through sabbaticals and other needs.

Though this book focuses on congregationally based ministers, there are others who also fall in the categories of minister who should consider sabbaticals: judicatory officials, chaplains, church school administrators, and others can all benefit from the renewal sabbatical affords. Though they may be less likely to have sabbatical opportunities, by all means they should consider negotiating with their institutions for leave opportunities.

In churches where there is no sabbatical policy, it is usually left to the pastor to broach the subject. Often, this does not happen until the need for time away has become serious, if not severe.

In his last book, the late spiritual leader Henri Nouwen wrote about his own sabbatical year. I read his book *Sabbatical Journey* during my clergy leave. Nouwen was suffering from great fatigue throughout this last year of his life, likely a sign that he needed medical attention, since he died only a few weeks after returning to his pastoral work at the L'Arche Daybreak Community in Toronto.[5] Even so, the book was a great lesson to me in how important it is for us to listen to our bodies. When we are fatigued, we need rest; when we are stressed, we need relief; when we are sick, we need to get well. Pastors, like everyone else, should pay attention to the signals our bodies send us. We need to realize how important it is to head off burnout before it gets a hold on us. By taking care of ourselves, we are also taking care of the churches who have called us.

Wheat Ridge Ministries is an organization that helps Lutherans seed new ministries of health and hope. Among its interests is health and wholeness among clergy and members of congregations. Wheat Ridge vice president Richard Herman sees sabbatical as "an intentional tool to combat the tendency to work at the expense of health." When congregations see their pastor as a person with spiritual and physical needs of rest and renewal, they may recognize the need for sabbath in their own lives and work.

This is what sabbatical is about: health, wholeness, and renewal. These things give clergy like me the opportunity to restart ministry in the same location.

For Inspiration

Both before and during my sabbatical, I found keeping a journal helped me sort out my thoughts, struggles, and dreams. Many people of faith over the centuries have used a journal for the same purpose. The good thing about a journal is its complete privacy unless the writer decides to reveal its contents to others. One need not be a professional writer to find journal keeping a helpful spiritual and emotional exercise.

If you have not kept a journal recently, why not consider starting now? All you need is paper and a writing implement. You can even use your word processor. Just find a quiet place and time and begin to record your thoughts. A journal may, of course, include the events around you, but mostly it is about what is going on *within* you. And you don't have to keep up with your journal writing on a daily basis. Write when something is troubling or thrilling you, or when you simply feel like doing so.

Since you are reading this book, it is likely you have experienced some need for renewal in your life and work. Why not write a journal entry about that need? What do you dream about in terms of renewal? What is holding you back? With whom do you need to talk in order to make renewal happen? What spiritual needs lie under the surface of your desires?

For Contemplation

Is there a particular scripture passage you always turn to when you are in need of renewal? Psalm 42 begins: "As a deer longs for flowing streams, so my soul longs for you, O God. My soul thirsts for God, for the living God" (vv. 1-2a).

Think about the ways your soul longs for God, and the ways in which your thirst for God is not being quenched. In your prayer today, don't worry so much about talking to God, but sit quietly and allow God's spirit to come to you. Simply rest and relax in the presence of God. Begin to allow God to quench your thirst and satisfy your spiritual hunger.

For Action

1. Don't wait for a sabbatical to find renewal. In addition to the ideas mentioned above, think deeply about the things that will bring you renewal now. More time with your family or friends? Rediscovering silence? Walks in nature? Make a move toward accomplishing one of those things.
2. If sabbatical is a goal, start now to talk about it with those who are important to you or can help make it happen: family; friends; spiritual advisor; judicatory officials; other clergy.
3. If you are feeling the effects of what you guess may be stress or burnout, get help. Don't wait.
    a. See your doctor to rule out any physical problems. Continue to get regular checkups.
    b. Consider starting yoga or some other relaxation technique to help you counter the effects of stress.
    c. Begin or renew a healthy exercise program after checking with your doctor. Exercise is essential to combating stress.
    d. Eat healthfully.

For Further Study

About keeping a journal:

Johnson, Alexandra. *Leaving a Trace: On Keeping a Journal.* Boston: Little, Brown, and Company, 2002.

Klug, Ronald. *How to Keep a Spiritual Journal: A Guide to Journal Keeping for Inner Growth and Personal Discovery.* Minneapolis: Augsburg, 1993.

Peace, Richard. *Spiritual Journaling: Recording Your Journey toward God.* Colorado Springs: NavPress, 1998.

About Clergy Self-care:

Oswald, Roy M. *Clergy Self-Care: Finding a Balance for Effective Ministry.* Washington, D.C: The Alban Institute, 1991.

Melander, Rochelle, and Harold Eppley. *The Spiritual Leader's Guide to Self-Care*. Bethesda, Md.: The Alban Institute, 2002.

About Sabbaticals:

Nouwen, Henri J. M. *Sabbatical Journey: The Diary of His Final Year*. New York: Crossroad, 1998.

Chapter 2

What To Do?

Journal: Deciding How to Spend My Time

Summer 2001

A phone call I made this week has me rethinking my interests and motives. In late spring of this year I had pointed out a news article to our church's session [governing board] about clergy renewal grants for sabbaticals. Almost apologetically, I mentioned it might be too good an opportunity for us to miss. I say "apologetically" because a sabbatical would mean my being away from the congregation for several months, and I was not sure how the idea would be received.

Since I have always made sure my continuing education programs were in fields that would benefit the congregation and not just benefit me, I asked the members of the session to think about a possible focus for a time of clergy renewal, should we consider applying. The next month, the personnel committee returned with a suggestion: they would like me to pursue the grant in order to write children's stories. One of my tiny "claims to fame" in the congregation is a series of children's sermons that revolve around a couple of dogs who are always getting into fixes and learning about life and God. People have encouraged me to write and submit them for publication, but I cannot seem to make the time in my regular schedule. We all decided I would pursue the sabbatical grant, with the idea of using the time to write my children's sermons in some publishable form. I have long wanted to pursue writing, and it seemed as though this might be just the right beginning.

Time passed and the deadline for submitting applications grew closer, and still I had not made the call. I was busy. I was a commissioner to our denomination's General Assembly, which required a great deal of reading and preparation, not to mention a week in California at meetings. While I was there, Jerry was in an accident and I came home early to care for him. All this was on top of my regular responsibilities as solo pastor.

Nevertheless, I realized this week the deadline was nearly upon us, and I finally made the call. I reached a recording stating applications for the grants were no longer available since the deadline was so near.

I had missed it.

Since that day, I have been kicking myself for waiting so long. I am not a procrastinator by nature. Why did I put off this important call? Being busy is only a partial answer.

Today I am beginning to formulate a few possible answers to this question. First, though I like the concept of writing the children's stories, I cannot seem to generate much personal energy around it. The thought of spending three months or so on that project alone makes me feel tired. There are other things—many other things—that intrigue me more. It has taken me until now to articulate this, even to myself.

Second, I have not had (or made) time to let the idea of sabbatical ferment in my mind as to what *would* energize me in the continuation of this long pastorate. The possibility of a sabbatical seems like a good idea, but what would it mean for me? What would it mean for the congregation? How would it work? I am a person who likes to do research on a project before beginning it, and I have done none on this one. I am not ready. To begin something and feel unprepared for what would come is far out of my comfort zone. I need to do some reading, ask questions, and, most importantly, spend time in thought and prayer about my own needs and desires. As well intentioned as the personnel committee's suggestion was, I have to think about what I want to do.

Finally, I think I am actually afraid of spending that much time away from the congregation. What if I become bored or purposeless (which may indeed happen if I choose to write the children's stories and nothing else)? What if difficult issues arise in the church while I am gone? What if—and this is a big what if—I find I like it so much I don't want to return?

This last thought is a revelation to me. I did not even know it was lurking in my psyche until I began to write it. It just seems to show, however, I am indeed in need of some type of renewal. I have become tired in my work. I rarely have time for real reflection, my sermons continue to feel dry, my enthusiasm for work in this wonderful congregation has waned.

I know I need something. I will continue to explore possibilities of sabbatical, and I will think about what would energize my work. There is always next year, and I certainly can hang on that long.

September 2000

With September has come, unexpectedly, a new round of applications for a clergy renewal grant for sabbaticals.

Since my last reflections on the idea of sabbatical, I have thought much about the concept and how it might apply to me. Did I think it was worthwhile to spend a few months away from the congregation? How would I spend that time? As I said in an earlier entry, I have up until now only participated in continuing education activities I thought would benefit the church, often rejecting ones that sounded incredibly interesting to me when church results seemed less obvious. Now, though, I am beginning to think a little more selfishly about the idea of renewal. Could it be that finding something which delights and renews me, without thinking so much about what the members of the congregation would like, could actually help them by helping me? Might personal renewal lead to renewal in the work I do in the church?

January 2001

It has done me good to apply for a grant, because the very act of writing the application has made me clarify what it is I need and want. What I need is renewal; there is no question. I need renewal in my work, my sense of call, and my life as pastor. I need renewed creativity, above all. When I imagined what would bring me the most energy during a sabbatical, and allowed my thoughts to ferment over a few months, I arrived at a surprisingly complex answer. I would enjoy writing, though not really with a specific project in mind, and I would like to learn photography. In addition, I have always wanted to travel to Scotland, and hiking in the mountains brings me as much joy as anything. Through all those activities, and in the rest and renewal they bring, I want to spend time reconnecting with God.

For almost as long as I can remember, I have wanted to explore the art of making pictures. It would be difficult to draw a direct line between photography and my work as pastor. On the other hand, I think what I am in need of more than any other asset right now is a new boost of creativity. Why couldn't flexing some new creative muscle help to bring the rest of my atrophying creativity new strength?

So, here is my goal: fifteen weeks of sabbatical in the fall of the year (my favorite season) to sharpen the craft of writing and to learn the art of photography. I would like to take a course in each area. Then I would spend the rest of the time honing those skills at home, spending time with Jerry, traveling, hiking, and recovering my spiritual self.

Choosing a Focus for the Sabbatical

Deciding how I might spend three months of clergy renewal time was a process for me. I moved from the expectations of others to daydreaming about what would fulfill my own needs and desires. Richard Bruesehoff, director of leadership support for the Evangelical Lutheran Church in America, tells pastors to imagine, "What will make your heart sing?" and to see what ideas germinate from the seeds of imagination. That question leads to other questions, he says: "What will bring you joy?" and "What will give you the courage to be a part of change?" when you return to the life of a pastor after the sabbatical ends.[1]

A sabbatical is primarily for the renewal of the pastor, but when the pastor is rejuvenated, so is the congregation. As change occurs in the pastor, leading from weariness to energy, from same-old to newness, from overwork to rest, that change almost of necessity seeps from the pastor's life into the church's life. We are not beings who live apart from our work; rather, who we are greatly affects what we do. Both the positive and negative aspects of our "pastoral personality" are contagious in the congregation. Therefore, what gives us joy in renewal most likely will assist us in being agents of positive change upon our return.

According to Bill Brosend, associate director for the Louisville Institute (who is also a former American Baptist pastor who benefited from a sabbatical), "Careful planning is essential. Successful sabbaticals include time for study, reflection and prayer, time for family, time to explore other churches, traditions, and religious practices, and ample time for nothing. The nothing is especially important at the beginning and end of the sabbatical period."

It's important, then, not to *over*plan. You are looking for renewal, not looking to do as much as possible in the amount of time given. If there is not time to rest and regain some sense of the sacredness of your life and work, then you may simply be trading one overly scheduled calendar for another, and may return after the sabbatical with no renewed vision or call.

For every pastor, the question of what to do with clergy renewal time will be answered differently. Presbyterian pastor Thom Shuman started thinking about sabbatical in a casual conversation with a church member. The church's governing body was very receptive to the idea, then

> I realized I had to give some serious thought to what might take place. If I had the chance to take off for three months, and do whatever I wanted and go wherever I wanted, what would it be? Well, as much as I hate to fly, I discovered what I really wanted to do was to visit and stay at some of those religious communities whose liturgy and resources have been shaping my personal life, as well as our congregational life, over the last ten years. I would visit Iona, Taizé, and the Northumbria Community overseas, and finally make a journey to the Abbey of Gethsemani which I had talked so much about visiting.

Others had similar experiences of reflecting, but came to far different conclusions for the execution of their time. Mark Asman, an Episcopal priest from California, had thought for some time about what he might do with a sabbatical. He spent three months in Mexico, delighting in a completely different culture and context, studying at the seminary in Mexico City and working for an ecumenical network with the gay and lesbian community there, then he spent one final month traveling in the United States. Methodist pastor Mike Mather chose to spend six months with his wife and children. For six weeks they traveled in India and Bangladesh; they spent three months at a conference center in New Mexico (the children attended school there); finally they took a month to travel slowly home by way of visiting friends and family and several western national parks. Lutheran pastor David Holte traveled with his family and built a deck on his home. Rabbi Michael Cohen lived and taught in Israel for a year. Linda Johnson, an Episcopal priest, went to Salisbury, England, to study 19th-century tracts and sermons.

The point is, you will know what will renew you. You may need to dig deep, as I did, to allow yourself to dream. On the other hand, like some of the others mentioned above, your dreams may be closer to the surface and you already know.

One thing is nearly certain: You will come back a different person to your congregation if you allow this time to change you. And, if both they and you are open, the renewing changes in you will help to effect change in the congregational system as well.

For Inspiration

If you are sensing the need for sabbatical, inspiration may feel like something in the past. Or it may be that you simply desire to be closer to God in new ways. Is there a particular place where you sense the presence of God more acutely? The church sanctuary? A hammock in your backyard? A nearby park? A spot in your own home? Go to that place and simply rest in God's presence.

For your journal, write about your fears (or enthusiasm) on leaving the congregation's work in the hands of the laity in your absence. Is this keeping you from pursuing sabbatical? Is it pushing you forward?

For Contemplation

In the last chapter, I suggested you find a way to get renewal now, without waiting for sabbatical. While keeping that idea in mind and acting on it, begin to plan what you might do with renewal time if you are given the opportunity. Use your own daydreams as your primary resource. Rather than worrying about what your church wants you to do (or what you *think* they want you to do), think creatively about what would bring you renewal.

When I was working through my application process for my sabbatical, I let the church know what was going on. A friend came to my office one day with a booklet she had made which described "out-of-the-box" ideas I might consider. (One I remember was an alpaca trek up Machu Picchu!) Her booklet was one more encouragement to allow myself to dream, and it helped me down the road of creative thinking. Here is my own list of ideas to get you started down the same road. It is by no means intended to limit or even direct, but to help you open up your own daydreaming.

- Visit the Holy Land
- Participate in an archaeological dig
- Learn conversational Italian

- Ride a bike across your state
- Read all the sermons of John Wesley
- Hike the Appalachian Trail
- Learn about another religion
- Take a class in Thai cooking
- Join a rowing team
- Work on a Habitat for Humanity project from beginning to end
- Train for a marathon
- Spend a month in a homeless shelter
- Sharpen your tennis game
- Begin an oral history of your family
- Build a canoe with your grandchild
- Write a memoir of your growing-up years
- Visit a site important to your faith tradition
- Eat lunch every day with your family
- Make a month-long visit to a monastery
- Enroll in a seminary class
- Study mathematics
- Explore the unity between faith and science

For Action

If you are serious about taking a sabbatical, now is the time to move ahead in the planning process. Talk to the appropriate group (governing board, personnel committee, pastor–parish relations committee) about your needs and desires. Be specific. Tell them why this is important for both you and the congregation (see the next chapter for specific information about benefits to the church). You may wish to have someone talk to them for you: a judicatory official or a pastor who has taken a sabbatical.

For Further Study

The most helpful resource I have seen is *Clergy Renewal: The Alban Guide to Sabbatical Planning* by A. Richard Bullock and Richard J. Bruesehoff (Bethesda, Md.: The Alban Institute, 2000); see especially chapter four. This book was very helpful to me in my own planning process.

Make a field trip to your favorite bookstore when you have a couple of hours to spare. Spend time in the periodicals section, just browsing in your favorite subject areas. Pick up a couple of periodicals that grab your attention and look in the back for advertisements or trips, classes, schools, projects. What strikes a chord in you?

Chapter 3

The Congregation Needs a Sabbatical, Too

Journal: Beyond Myself

January 31, 2001

One of the best things we have done so far as our session considers a sabbatical has been the openness of our process. I have encouraged the session members to discuss the idea openly with others, I've mentioned it from the pulpit several times, and there have been articles in the newsletter. In each case we have asked for feedback and have encouraged people to come to us with their questions and concerns.

This past Sunday was our annual meeting, and I admit to being a little nervous because the sabbatical was to be the main topic for discussion. To my surprise, the members present seemed unanimously supportive of our exploring a grant for clergy renewal leave. One thing that helped, I believe, was our having prepared a very specific plan of what would happen in the congregation during my absence. The chairs of the personnel and worship committees and I have already met with Florence Beaujon, a retired pastor who would lead worship and spend a couple of days in the office each week. She's a good fit for our congregation, and I suspect (hope) she has a very different pastoral style from mine. It will benefit all of us if the church experiences a new style. After nine years, surely it is a good thing to experience the fresh perspective of an outsider. I can't possibly be the only one who is tired of my creativity slump.

Additionally, several of our members met Florence at a meeting held at our church not that long ago, so she is not completely unknown to them. That fact makes many people breathe easier. Fifteen weeks sounds like a long time if it's to be spent with someone you're not sure about.

It is important to the session and to me that the congregation not just mark time for those 15 weeks, and so we have also considered not only what I might do with the time, but what they might do with it. How could it be a time of *mutual* learning, reflection, increased creativity, and renewal?

One of our members once attended an event about spiritual gifts, and also remembers hearing Florence say she has a particular interest in helping church members discover and use their gifts. So we've pursued this avenue with her. Our hope is she will preach a series of sermons and conduct other events around this theme. Since this is a subject I've never seriously tackled, it should be a delightful departure from the ordinary. Florence seems genuinely enthused, as does the congregation.

I am very grateful to have been in this place for nine years, but I continue to worry about things like complacency and growing stale—not just myself, but also the church. We have been blessed with vital church members, but I sometimes get concerned about our willingness to continue doing things the same old way. Ideas we have worked on together since I arrived have now become "the way we've always done it." Some projects and programs, once exciting and new, now need reworking. Sabbatical may just give us the opportunity to step back from the ordinary, see ourselves and our calling in a slightly different light, and imagine what the next years together might hold.

Being in a church where there is mutual affection between pastor and congregation has many obvious benefits for both. We have become comfortable working together, trust each other's opinions and observations, expect the best from one another, forgive easily when there are difficulties. On the other hand, such a relationship is in danger of becoming so easy that neither party wants to offend the other by suggesting something new, or to rock the comfort boat by stepping off in a different direction from before.

I want us to be able to continue to capitalize on all those benefits, while learning to listen together for God's new call to us. Where should we go next? What will our dreams be? How will we realize them? Who will help us move ahead? How can we be both truthful and hopeful about the future?

At our annual meeting, we discussed these big-picture reasons for having a sabbatical, and also dealt with very concrete concerns about how the church will function without its regular pastor for more than three months. Since I am a solo pastor, this may be a more important issue here than for a congregation with a large staff. We were able to talk about these concerns openly and candidly. We have some work cut out for us in the months ahead.

More and more I have come to believe a sabbatical may give all of us a chance to step back from each other, reevaluate our work in this place, and renew our sense of call to each other and to our particular place. I hope our absence from each other will renew not just me as the pastor, but the work of the church as a whole. People may find something in the temporary arrangement that is refreshing and interesting. They may think of ways to integrate the new into the old. They may dream of creating something completely different out of what has been the same for some time. This is my hope.

Why the Congregation Needs You to Go Away for a While

Don't take it personally, but your congregation needs you to leave. Not forever, but for a few weeks or months. Why? Because while you are gone, they will learn all sorts of things about themselves they may have forgotten since you arrived. They may suddenly remember how to work the thermostats, when the building needs to be unlocked for the scout troop, how to plan worship, whose turn it is to make the coffee before the service, and when to start organizing the fall stewardship campaign. More importantly, they may remember to visit and care for each other, how to make visitors feel welcome, and that someone needs to stay in contact with the local food pantry. It will be good for them to remember these things without your prompting.

Recently I met a pastor who said to me, "There is no way I could ever take a sabbatical. If I'm gone for just one week the whole place falls apart." It seems to me this congregation and its pastor may have an unhealthy dependence. Each needs to learn the future is not dependent upon the other. If the pastor became sick, the church would survive. If the church closed its doors, the pastor would survive. They need to choose to continue their life together because they want to, not because they feel stuck in dependence. Sabbatical can provide the self-differentiation they need by giving them time apart to remember who they are without the other.

The whole ministry of your congregation may be revitalized by your absence. Though that thought may be hard for us pastors to take, just imagine all the things you do and how much you and the congregation take for granted in each other. When that comfortable operating system is disturbed, God may just find a few more ears who are willing to listen for the stirring of the Spirit.

Judicatory executive Cheryl Ann Elfond sees the sabbatical as "a time to focus learning and also help the congregation move forward," assisting in the congregation's ability to see "itself as capable and intentional in its own development." How else will folks remember they can do ministry unless you go away?

Understandably, there will be concerns in the congregation (and likely also in the mind of the pastor) about how things will go during the sabbatical. Will attendance and giving drop? Who will handle the workload? Who will handle funerals, weddings, and baptisms? Among the pastors and officials I interviewed, the three "hot button issues" most commonly mentioned as concerns among members were: (1) Will the pastor come back? (2) Where will we get the money? and (3) How will we manage?

These concerns must be addressed realistically and up front. It may help to have a judicatory official come to one of your governing board or congregational meetings to talk about how other churches like yours have handled sabbatical planning and difficulties. Another excellent resource might be a nearby pastor and lay leader from a congregation that has profited from a pastoral sabbatical. The lay leader can vouch for the benefits to the whole organization, as well as talk about what happened in the pastor's absence.

You will want a written sabbatical policy. The best situation is when the sabbatical is in the terms of the original call, but most congregations and pastors don't look that far ahead, for a variety of reasons. Sometimes, interim pastors can lay the groundwork for sabbatical. Harris Schultz, a trainer of interims, urges congregations and their search committees to consider including a sabbatical in the initial contract. Many judicatory officials told me they thought such a provision in the contract would give congregations an edge in an increasingly competitive search process.

It is not too late, though, to write a policy for the sabbatical you are planning. It is a perfect way, in addition to public meetings, announcements, and newsletter articles, to address the "hot button issues" mentioned earlier.

Regarding those issues, the pastor must be willing to give assurances in writing of the plan to return for at least a year following the sabbatical. If the pastor is unwilling to do this, the congregation will be more anxious both during and after the sabbatical, and may be less than willing to allow the time away. Second, money matters will need to be addressed (since this is so important and often difficult, I will address it at length in the next chapter). At the very least, though, the policy will state that the church will maintain the normal salary and benefits to the pastor during the sabbatical. And third, pastor and governing board together should develop a plan for managing in the pastor's absence.

Roy Oswald has produced a video presentation, *Why You Should Give Your Pastor a Sabbatical*, in which he approaches the subject from the congregation's point of view and lists many benefits.[1] In addition, the book *Clergy Renewal* by Richard Bullock and Richard Bruesehoff gives a variety of practical suggestions for sabbatical planning.[2] Both resources are appropriate for viewing or studying with a governing board. It is extremely important to work through appropriate channels in informing and preparing the congregation. Sabbath leave is an important matter, and people need to know it is being done right.

Bullock and Bruesehoff give a "Who Does What" sample plan in an appendix. It addresses the responsibilities normally filled by the pastor and who will fill them during the sabbatical. A judicatory or other congregation near you may have worked out a plan you will want to adapt for your purposes.

While we speak of all the benefits to a congregation when the pastor takes a sabbatical, let us not encourage the congregation to expect too much in terms of a product of sorts when the pastor returns. The "product" may be new vision, renewed spiritual depth, a determination to lead the congregation through needed change. Those are hardly things that can be quantified, yet they are invaluable to a congregation's health, wholeness, and future. The Louisville Institute's Bill Brosend says that it is "important not to 'oversell' the sabbatical with promises of all the wonderful benefits parishioners should expect as a result of granting time for sabbatical. In fact, for the most part the benefits are secondary and tangential—the fruits of being led by a pastoral leader whose vocation and spirit have been renewed, rather than primary and central 'benefits' like a new program, initiative, or innovation in the life of the church. And that is okay."

Congregations have used the sabbatical time in as many ways as there are situations. Yes, some only mark time until the pastor's return. I suspect these congregations will be less enthused about sabbatical the next time around. On the other hand, others find they learn to know an associate or temporary pastor and develop a much deeper relationship with that person. Some create new strategies for visiting the sick and shut-ins. Some experiment with new programs or complete a remodeling project. Most find they have to encourage more lay involvement, and very many gain a new appreciation of the diversity of pastoral tasks. Nearly all discover they can survive—even thrive—without the pastor. Arthur Boers was happy to hear that summer attendance, which usually slumped, was up when members took on preaching assignments in his absence.

Not a small matter is realizing that the minister's renewal is good for the church. Lutheran synod bishop Peter Rogness says about the benefits of sabbaticals: "Congregations received back a minister refreshed personally, emotionally, spiritually, and with some fresh ideas for congregational life. Congregations themselves view the minister differently—more positively—after an extended absence." Not only does the congregation learn it can thrive in the pastor's absence, it also discovers the delight of welcoming a "new" pastor in the person of the "old" one.

Lutheran pastor David Holte says about his return from sabbatical, "I think it was good for the congregation to discover how wonderfully well they can do without me around every day." If we are to have healthy pastors and healthy congregations, such a discovery is good for us all.

For Inspiration

How is your thinking and praying already being transformed by the idea of renewal and by the steps toward renewal you have already taken? Find in the scriptures a story or passage that exemplifies your spiritual longings or renewal, and use it as the foundation for 10 minutes of quiet meditation.

In your journal, reflect on the strengths and weaknesses of the congregation.

For Contemplation

1. Put away, for a moment, your own need for renewal, and think about the ways in which the congregation you serve needs to be revitalized. How might such revitalization be aided by and begin during your absence? How might the members and the organization grow and benefit? In what ways have they become too dependent on your leadership? What style of preaching, administration, or pastoral care would be good for them to experience?
2. As you have read this chapter, what "hot button issues," if any, do you think will be set off in your congregation as the subject of sabbatical is broached? What resources will you use to educate the members and to allay any fears?

For Action

Now is the time to develop a strategy for introducing the concept of sabbatical to the congregation. What appropriate levels of your structure need to be informed/consulted? For instance, in my setting I worked with the personnel committee, who took the idea to our governing board. Only when they were in full support did we together go to the congregation.

Discuss your strategy with someone else, perhaps a leader in your judicatory, and solicit help at all the important points of the process.

Allow at least six months, preferably a year before the beginning of your sabbatical, to prepare the congregation and finalize your plan. The Oswald video is especially helpful for personnel committees and governing boards. It gives many important reasons why it is good for the congregation to give the pastor a sabbatical. Be ready for questions afterward.

Give your own personal narrative about why you think a sabbatical is important and appropriate at this particular time. This will be the hardest part for many of you. (Aren't pastors supposed to be selfless?) Here's a good time to bring in someone from the outside who has taken a sabbatical, along with a lay leader from a congregation that has reaped the benefits. Let them tell their story and respond to concerns from your board or committee.

Put together a proposed sabbatical policy. Ideally, this would have happened when your call originated at the current congregation. Even so, now is a good time. It should delineate how long the sabbatical will be (include dates), and a promise from you of at least one year beyond the end of the leave. It will also include continuation of your full salary and benefits. A sabbatical generally does not include regular vacation and/or study leave time. These are considered to be separate from the sabbatical.

Begin working with the appropriate group on a specific plan. What will be the design for congregational learning? Who will cover which responsibilities? What will happen if there is a death, marriage, or baptism in the congregation? Who will lead the confirmation class, visit the sick and elderly, administer the sacraments, and teach the Thursday morning Bible study?

For Further Study

In addition to the video and book footnoted in this chapter, ask around about copies of sabbatical policies and plans. I have included a policy from one judicatory here. In this particular policy, the church is responsible for the continuation of the pastor's salary and benefits, but not for additional costs incurred (except for continuing education funds so applied). See the next chapter for other financial options.

SABBATICAL PROGRAM
A Policy of the Heartland Presbytery, Presbyterian Church (USA)

The purpose of a sabbatical program is to provide, in cooperation with the session of the congregations involved, an opportunity for qualified pastors to spend three months away from the parish and its duties. The program provides for the pastor selected to engage in a program of study and growth experiences as approved by the pastor's session. This sabbatical program would provide the pastor with an opportunity for increased skill development and restorative growth experiences in a setting entirely free from the demands of the parish.

It provides also for a method of continuing pastoral and administrative functions for the congregation. At the end of the sabbatical, the pastor will return to the congregation renewed by the extended absence from regular pastoral pressures and by new insights and skills gained during the leave. It is hoped this approach will empower pastors to discover a newness in their professional calling and life that some pastors seek through a new call, even though they do not feel a need to move otherwise.

Arrangements
1. Congregations will continue to pay the pastor's salary, housing, major medical and pension during the sabbatical time.
2. Professional expenses (travel, meals, etc.) would not be paid.
3. Heartland Presbytery would provide assistance in locating a 20-hour a week supply pastor, if desired, utilizing available clergy from the Presbytery or Commissioned Lay Pastors, mutually agreeable to the Committee on Ministry and the session.
4. Pastors would apply the annual amount usually provided by the congregation for continuing education and/or books toward the cost of this program.
5. To qualify, pastors would have completed at least five years of continuing service to their particular congregation and

would agree to continue at least one additional year in the same location upon return.

6. A written report to the session and the Presbytery's Committee on Ministry of insights gained, experiences undertaken, and work/study completed would be required.

Chapter 4

Who Will Pay for This?

Journal: Where Will the Money Come From?

May 2001

I've been worried about what I'll do if our sabbatical grant doesn't come through. Since late last year my anticipation of sabbatical has grown so that I have lately begun to lie awake nights trying to come up with an alternative plan.

At the annual meeting one of our dear members said if we didn't receive the grant he thought we should go ahead with the plan anyway. I laughed then, knowing we could not come up with the amount of money in our grant request. Lately I haven't been laughing about it. I've been considering it.

We are a small church, with an annual budget of a little over $100,000. We maintain a 150-year-old building and we give as much as possible to mission. It is not possible for us, at least at this late date, to finance the $24,000-plus request we've made for a grant.

I'm kicking myself for not having started planning several years ago. I should have put something about sabbatical into my original terms of call, and we should have set aside some money every year. But we didn't.

Perhaps we can do some scaled-back version. Instead of hiring Florence for two days a week plus Sunday, maybe we can just get pulpit supply preachers for Sundays and rely more on the members of the congregation to do the pastoral work. Jerry and I can cut out the trip to Scotland, and I can buy a used camera instead of a new one. Maybe I can find writing and photography courses closer to home, to save money on airfare. Certainly I can use my continuing education money to fund some of the expenses. Ah, well. At the very least, if there is no grant we can begin planning for next year.

May 17, 2001

A few minutes before choir practice the phone at church rang. It was a representative of the Lilly Endowment, informing us our grant application was accepted. I'm going on sabbatical!

Funding Your Sabbatical

One of the main questions of pastors and congregations around the subject of clergy renewal is, "How are we going to afford this?" It is a good question, and it has many answers. Sadly, it is a question that sometimes stops the discussion altogether. The question of funding has, in many churches, kept the congregation and pastor from pursuing the good things a sabbatical can offer. Then again, money is often a difficult issue, not just around sabbaticals but around lots of other programs and concerns as well.

    If we believe sabbaticals are good for everyone concerned, then we should be willing to invest time and creativity into their funding. Money should not stop churches from supporting clergy renewal. There are many, many possibilities. In my interviews for this book, I talked with pastors who received $30,000 grants, and I talked with pastors who received nothing outside their regular salary. Though the money (or lack of it) affected what they did during their sabbatical, it did not seem to affect the value of that time.

Here again, it is wise if a sabbatical policy is in place early in the pastor's relationship with a congregation. That way, funding can be discussed up front, and money can be set aside in a special fund each year. When the sabbatical time arrives, the fund is already complete. Even if such a policy was not established at the beginning, the governing board can start the fund as soon as the concept of sabbatical is approved, giving time for it to accumulate.

Money, in almost every congregation, is an important issue. Sometimes it is a volatile one, as members or groups struggle over limited resources. So many important ministries, projects, and programs vie for dollars. Still, if clergy renewal is important, a congregation can find creative ways of funding it.

Any church should be able to continue the pastor's salary and benefits during the weeks and months of renewal. They would be paying it anyway, so continuing it because the pastor is not physically in the building should not be a financial strain.

A major financial consideration for the congregation concerns obtaining pastoral skills. Some churches with a pastoral staff simply spread the work out among the remaining staff members. Some reworking of job descriptions might have to be done for the short term so the staff is not overworked. They should not resent the staff member who is gone. For an associate pastor, it can be excellent experience to take on extra roles and duties. Often, staff members will be glad to fill out the required duties, especially if they know their turn for sabbatical will come someday.

Other churches have delighted in having a different preacher every Sunday, either a supply preacher (usually at a reasonable cost) or various members of the congregation (at no cost). Perhaps your denomination, like mine, has lay pastors who have been trained by your judicatory, or there may be a retired minister locally. You will also need to have someone lined up to handle pastoral emergencies like funerals and hospital visitation. Look to the folks who help you out when you are on vacation; they may be delighted to fill in, expecting you will do the same for them some day. Lay people can handle many pastoral duties, and you may find them more willing to continue in some new roles when you return once they have had a chance to see how rewarding such work can be. None of these alternatives is very expensive.

The earlier you plan, the better off you are. Might your members get excited over the possibility of learning new skills? You could plan a class for preachers, teaching some of your lay people how to prepare and deliver sermons. A visitation ministry can be developed if there is enough time, allowing members to learn to care for each other pastorally. Look around you and see the latent gifts of the members. What a wonderful time to encourage people to spread their wings and share their gifts with other people.

Now, who will pay for your extra expenses? You want to travel to some exotic location, purchase books and equipment, learn a new skill, study at a university. All of these cost money. Nearly every year, it seems, there are new possibilities for clergy renewal grants (you will find a listing of some of them at the end of this chapter). Check with your judicatory and denomination for additional funding. Ask the financial aid department of the institution where you want to study. Find out if there are scholarships available for conferences. Use frequent flier miles.

Get the congregation involved in creative financing. Some airlines allow customers to give their frequent flier miles to others; perhaps several members together could come up with enough miles for a trip. Or maybe someone in the congregation has a second residence in another location they would be willing to lend to you for a few weeks. How about a fund raiser for the purpose of financing the sabbatical?

Generally, granting institutions will have specific requirements and application processes to follow. You will need to obtain information from them well ahead of time (I suggest an initial contact at least one year ahead of your planned leave). The Lilly Endowment of Indianapolis, Indiana, is a relatively new and excellent resource for clergy renewal grants. Each year since 1999 the Endowment has given 30 grants to Indiana congregations and up to 100 grants in their national program, for as much as $30,000 each. Jean M. Smith, an Endowment program director for religion, says the grants are designed for churches whose pastors have been in their current positions for several years. "One of the purposes of the grants," according to Smith, "is to support clergy in long-term pastorates through a self-directed program of renewal and refreshment." (See the information at the end of this chapter to learn more about grant possibilities.)

You should have some ideas together about financing before going to the church board to propose a sabbatical, since they will likely be asking you about money. Have a list of grants you may apply for, and a back-up list of other options.

If you don't receive a grant and still don't have enough money, consider scaling back what you would like to do. Renewal was so important to me I was willing to forego the costly parts of my sabbatical and negotiate with my session for some money to put together a package for supply preachers, while using my continuing education money for travel and study expenses. I was willing to give up the most expensive parts of the proposal in order to have the *time*. For most of us, time is the most important aspect of renewal. Ellen Acton, an associate pastor, decided that all she and the church could afford was one month, so she decided to make the most of it. Though she probably needed and could have used more time, the month was renewing for her, and she returned refreshed after her limited time away.

Sabbath is, after all, a concept of time. There will be more about this later in the book. For now, it is enough to say that as you consider renewal, remember that time is the most healing and important part of a worthwhile sabbatical.

Whatever you do, don't give up the idea of renewal because of the money. Your congregation needs you to be renewed and they will be willing to work with your reasonable requests. If you don't have much money to work with, then you will just need to be more creative with your renewal plan. Meet with a colleague and brainstorm inexpensive ideas that will bring you joy and renewal.

Then, when you return from your sabbatical a new person, start planning the money for the next one.

For Inspiration

Go to your "stewardship" file or locate some of your denomination's stewardship materials. Read the scripture passages about money, time, and gifts. If you truly believe a sabbatical will be as beneficial for your congregation as for you, how can your resources and theirs be best used for this time?

Write in your journal about your relationship to money. How, as a pastor, has money helped or hindered your ministry? What resources in addition to finances are valuable to you, and how have you leaned upon them in the past? What aspects of personal and congregational stewardship are easy or difficult for you?

For Contemplation

1. How can your congregation come to understand that spending money on a sabbatical is as important as other spending decisions they will make (for education, the building, paying down the debt, etc.)?
2. Why would a granting institution be inclined to give money to you or your congregation? What do you have to offer, or what can you learn during a sabbatical that will make a difference?

For Action

1. Come up with a tentative funding plan for your sabbatical *before* you approach your governing board with the concept. You may want to talk to other pastors who have taken sabbaticals, or with your judicatory executive. Make a list of granting institutions to which you plan to apply. Have a back-up plan if the grants do not come through.
2. Investigate grants (see below for some information). Find out if your denomination has money available for sabbaticals.

3. Think with your church's finance committee about various avenues for funding, and creative ways of receiving the money you need.

For Further Study

For some good reflection on pastoral attitudes about money, see Dan Hotchkiss, *Ministry and Money: A Guide for Clergy and Their Friends* (Bethesda, Md.: The Alban Institute, 2002).

Below are some options for funding sources, adapted from a list on the Web site of CHARIS Ecumenical Center, Concordia College, Moorhead, Minnesota, www.cord.edu/dept/charis.

*   Bush Foundation
    The Bush Foundation in St. Paul has a "Leadership Fellows Program" that provides funding to support the educational goals of people so that they can serve more effectively as leaders in their communities and professions. Pastors are among those eligible. The fellowships are for periods from two to eighteen months, and persons aged 28 to 55. For more information, check their Web site at www.bushfoundation.org/index2.htm, or request information by e-mail (info@bushfoundation.org) or telephone (651-227-0891).

*   CrossCurrents Research Colloquium
    The Coolidge Fellows program awards grants for one-month study programs at a cluster of New York City schools: Union Theological Seminary, Auburn, Jewish Theological Seminary, Columbia University, Teachers College. The focus is on cross-cultural learning. Participants pay a registration fee and travel; the fellowship takes care of other costs. Contact: CrossCurrents, 29 Castle Place, New Rochelle, NY 10805. Requires a research or writing project. Web site: www.aril.org/colloquium.html.

*   Harvard Divinity School
    Ask about the Merrill Fellowship Program, which provides tuition and a stipend to cover expenses of room and board.

Four sabbatical fellowships offered each term. Recipients may study at Harvard or other affiliated schools of the Boston Theological Institute. Call: 617-496-2943.

- Lilly Endowment National Clergy Renewal Program
  A limited number of grants to Christian congregations and pastors with an M.Div. (grants are not available to those in noncongregational ministries). Please refer to the Endowment's Web site at www.clergyrenewal.org for current information on the program. Applicants should always be sure to use current application forms.

- The Louisville Institute
  The Louisville Institute (funded by Lilly Endowment Inc.) provides grants of $6,000 (six weeks), $8,000 (eight weeks), and $12,000 (twelve weeks) to pastors as part of their Sabbatical Grants for Pastoral Leaders program. Contact Dr. William Brosend by e-mail (info@louisville-institute.org) or call him at 502-895-3411, ext. 251.

- Pastor-Theologian Program
  This is not really a sabbatical program, but it is a program of extended study (three years), funded by Lilly Endowment Inc. and centered at Princeton Theological Seminary. This is a quite demanding program, but very good. Their Web site is www.ctinquiry.org or call 609-683-4797.

- The Presbyterian Church (U.S.A.) has a similar program of its own, also funded by the Lilly Endowment (for information, call 1-888-728-7228, ext. 5732).

- Benjamin N. Duke Fellowships
  To inquire about these fellowships for clergy sabbaticals at Duke Divinity School, call 919-660-3448 or send an e-mail to info@mail.duke.edu.

- The Proctor Scholarship
  The Episcopal Divinity School in Cambridge, Massachusetts
  has a scholarship for a one-semester residence for clergy and
  laity. Covers tuition, a single room, and 15 meals per week.
  Can include courses as well as individual study. For
  information, send an e-mail to amacione@episdivschool.org.

- Local sources
  Check with your judicatory for funding sources. Some have
  funds for this purpose; for instance, the Southeastern
  Minnesota Synod of the ELCA has had such a fund for some
  years, and the Wisconsin Conference of the UCC is using a
  "Forward in Faith Campaign" to, in part, fund sabbatical leaves
  for pastors in rural and smaller-membership churches. In
  addition, charitable and fraternal organizations (for Lutherans,
  local branches of Thrivent Financial for Lutherans) may also
  be able to supply such funds.

Chapter 5

It's Here. Now What?

Journal: The First Week

August 9, 2001 (Thursday)

Today I am halfway through the first week of my sabbatical. I wonder what other pastors who are taking leave think and feel during their first week. I doubt that any two of us experience the same things. For me, it has been both joyful and sad.

On Sunday, my last day in the pulpit for the next three-and-a-half months, I preached from the lectionary epistle reading, Colossians 3:1-11. In it, we read these words: "Set your minds on things that are above, not on things that are on earth . . . ." Though I doubt the author had sabbatical on his mind, the saying seems to apply to me and our congregation at this time.

I know I can sometimes get so caught up in the details of my job I sometimes forget the larger focus of my call. I do not think I am alone. Pastors have so many areas for which they are responsible, from calling the roofer when there is a leak to visiting people in the hospital, from counseling to planning a wedding, from preaching to writing an article for the newsletter. We expend all our energy on the necessary details, and we sometimes lose sight of the things that are above. I hope to be able during these next few months to lose myself in another world of writing, taking pictures, enjoying the outdoors, reading, and thinking so I can regain any lost sense of the big picture. It is not, I think, that I have lost my sense of call, either in general or to this specific congregation. Instead, I believe I can be renewed in understanding how the call will continue to carry me forward in this realm of daily details and work.

After worship on Sunday, the congregation gave me a send-off dinner and served many of my favorite foods. (Let me just say right here that if they gave me chocolate cheesecake every week I would not even be *thinking* sabbatical.) The meal was a kind and thoughtful way to say goodbye for a while and I was humbled to hear their words of encouragement and expectation. If there are members who think this renewal time is a bad idea, they have not mentioned it to me. Just the opposite has been true. Though they promise to miss me, to a person everyone has been extremely supportive.

When the meal was over I locked the church building and made one last trip to the hospital and nursing home, where we have some members who may not still be around in 15 weeks when I return. I have told their families that, if they wish, I will participate in any funerals that occur when I am not out of town. I know for some pastors that might be too much church contact during a sabbatical, but for me it seems the right thing to do. After nine-and-a-half years, these folks are my friends and mean a great deal to me. It would be an honor, not a burden, to officiate at their funerals. I had already told the ones who were cognizant that Sunday would be my last day for a while, so it was a series of bittersweet good-byes, as we wished each other well. Jerry keeps reminding me I can go see these folks any time I wish; it's not as though I have left the church for good. He's right, of course. I think I may find it difficult to know just how close or distant to remain.

Now it is Thursday, and I am in my fourth day of this experience/experiment. Some things are just as I had expected; others are not. I have not slept in or taken naps as I thought I might want to do the first weeks. Since Jerry continues with his regular schedule, I have arisen with him each morning so we can exercise together, just as we normally do. The difference for me, though, is I have a sense when we are jogging of the whole day stretched out in front of me, and I can do whatever I want with it. Usually my feeling is one of hurrying back so I can get to the church and get my work underway for the day.

On my day off last week, I set up my primary working space, which is one of the two desks in Jerry's home office. I sometimes work there when I have things to catch up on. On the desk was a gift from him: a blank journal in which to record my sabbatical reflections. I've tucked the note he wrote inside the front cover of the journal, so I can read it often. We have shared an office before, and so are not expecting to be faced with any issues of turf or too much togetherness. My laptop computer allows me to work in another room or on the porch when he's on the phone or if I just need a change of scenery.

As it has worked out, each day this week has been different. On Monday I started loaves of yeast bread before going to the office, then spent time getting settled and planning a general outline of what I would like to accomplish the first week. Tuesday I spent the day writing and reading. (I read an entire book! Do you know when was the last time I finished a book the same day I started it? Sure, it was a short book, but still . . .) Wednesday I ran errands and went out to lunch, coming back to work here mid-afternoon, and today I spent a couple of hours in the vegetable garden before hitting the office late morning. It has been a real delight to have a flexible schedule, and to allow myself to enjoy the flexibility without feeling guilty.

Another pleasure has been that of having time to spend with my daily devotions. I try to keep up with them regularly, but the time often, if not usually, feels hurried because of all the things calling to me from my "to-do" list. Now, it just does not matter how much time I take, because the whole day is before me to shape pretty much as I please.

One surprise has been that I have accomplished so much with such an unstructured schedule. My planner typically is quite full, with visits and appointments, and with rows of lists. This week my lists and their rows have been much shorter, and except for getting my hair cut, I have had no appointments. Theoretically, I might have just sat around and enjoyed the quiet, and that would have been fine. But I have been spurred to read and to write, and I am looking forward to what the next weeks will bring. Already, creativity seems to be returning to me.

Tomorrow is a packing day because I am leaving over the weekend to attend a conference for women writers in New York. I am thrilled about a whole week of being around people who are thinking about how to express themselves creatively. This is just what I have longed for.

If I had dreamed of the perfect first week of renewal, my dream would not have been any better than this.

Beginning Your Time Away

There are different kinds of sabbaticals, as many as there are different pastors. For some the time is simply that of rest. For others it is a time of study, either as part of a program or self-directed. For others it is a combination. If you choose to use part or all of your leave time for study, remember that study itself can be renewing. It may have been years, even decades, since you had the uninterrupted opportunity to delve into some subject deeply. Without the daily responsibilities of your work, now is the time for you to read, listen, explore, search. You can let your mind enter all those areas about which you had only longed to learn. Remember those days at seminary when certain thinkers or subjects captivated you? You can return to that sense of excited learning, but this time without being graded! According to Sam Roberson, a judicatory executive with the Presbyterian Church (USA), a sabbatical is "beneficial for pastors because it releases them from a routine and gives them permission to focus and think about things that otherwise they simply wouldn't get around to." That is the very definition of study and renewal.

Study can revolve around some issue in the congregation or simply something that interests you. Holly McKissick, a pastor serving greater Kansas City, spent part of her time reading in areas of personal interest, and another part in France and Italy studying the concept of sacred space, relating it to the building project at her home church.

Whatever you have chosen to do, there will come a time for separation from the congregation. For some this will be more difficult than for others. Planning is helpful here, because you can arrange with the governing board what your boundaries will be. Will you return for funerals? Will you be available for emergencies? Probably it is best to separate as much as possible. Once you have determined your boundaries, make them public and stick to them. If people call, refer them to the proper person designated to handle their area of concern. This is important, both for maintaining your ability to renew apart from the congregation and to keep members from being confused about what you will and will not do.

It is not only congregations who have trouble with boundaries and letting go; we pastors may have difficulty, too. It is necessary for you to let go of your responsibilities. Otherwise, you may find you are not really on leave at all, and your sabbatical will be less productive for you and for the congregation.

Most people find it helpful not to leave immediately on a major excursion the first day of the sabbatical. Instead, it seems wise to let sabbath begin gently, not in a rush. If sabbath is to have its effect on us, we need to give it time to do so.

I had expected to be exhausted my first week of sabbatical, or to feel at loose ends, but that was not the case. I was energized and excited about renewal possibilities. I teemed with ideas and enjoyed the moments as they presented themselves to me. The week was a wonderful surprise.

Some pastors I interviewed also found the beginnings of renewal to be refreshing. Others didn't quite know what to do with themselves. It can be difficult to slow down. Listen to these somewhat-typical words from Catholic priest Bill Schooler:

> As I left the parish and went to the airport, I had the distinct feeling that I was abandoning my flock. I was exhausted, after working overtime for weeks to get things ready. However, it did not take long for me to catch up on sleep and dismiss my feeling of guilt over abandoning my flock. There was no doubt in my mind that this was the right thing to do.

Many reported that the weeks preceding their leave-taking were jammed with extra preparations, training of others to fill in ministerial responsibilities, meetings, and even parties. Though necessary, these activities only add to the difficulty of getting away and should be spread out over as long a period as possible. Here is another reason for starting early in the sabbatical planning process. It's not desirable to be exhausted the first week of leave because of trying to get ready for leave!

As mentioned before, it is wise to meet early on with advisors, replacements, and lay leaders to decide how duties will be divided and who needs to be trained in what areas. Often the training itself can be shared among various people. Delegation over as wide a group as possible is an important way to keep from burning out a few active lay people or overloading the pastor's last few weeks before leaving.

When preparation has gone well and smoothly, the first weeks can be restful and reflective instead of time for recovery. Here are Dave Holte's thoughts on those beginning days:

> I clearly remember my feelings the first week. I felt freedom like I hadn't felt since high school—no schedule, no deadlines, no stress—it was wonderful. And I remember thinking that I was observing my own life and situation as an outsider, seeing things I hadn't seen while in the heat of work. "So this is how Dave lives. He has a beautiful family, he has it good, he has a beautiful home, etc." I know this sounds strange, but I noticed my life in a new and clear way because I had some time to reflect.

Time to reflect. Time. This is what clergy renewal is about. To continue in "the heat of work" our whole career is to rob ourselves and our congregations of the time we and they need to reflect on our lives and our call. Here is where change begins.

For Inspiration

Order an admissions catalog from a seminary you respect and look down their description of courses. If you were a student again, with unlimited study options, what courses would you take? Pick one or two. Is it possible to get a copy of the reading list for that course, or to create one yourself? Maybe this is a place to start for study renewal.

Write in your journal about the most renewing time you have experienced in your ministry. When was it? What about it revitalized you?

For Contemplation

Imagine how you would like to structure the first few weeks of your sabbatical. Will it be study, rest, travel, alone time, a combination? What plans do you need to make now?

Read a book or article about spirituality and determine to explore something new in your devotions for one month. Try Marjorie Thompson's *Soul Feast: An Invitation to the Christian Spiritual Life* (Louisville: Westminster John Knox, 1995) or another resource.

For Action

1. Your planning should be coming along well. Include firm boundaries about when and for what reasons you will be available, if at all. Make sure the governing board agrees with your boundaries and makes them public to the congregation. When it comes time to begin your leave, say goodbye and let go.
2. If reading is an important part of your renewal, begin to develop a reading plan. Will you set aside time each day or one or more days a week? Will certain weeks be devoted to reading and others to different activities? What kinds of topics will be the subject of your reading, or will you read a variety?

For Further Study

Here you will need to do your own research. Start a list of topics for reading, and then make a list of books to read under each topic. You can ask others who are knowledgeable in the particular field, do an internet search, or simply browse your local bookstore, library, or favorite book catalog. To get you started, here are some ideas. You may want to read in the field of:

- *Your favorite hobby or sport (or one you want to pursue).* Learn about building a wooden boat, sewing, bicycling, physical exercise and health program, pottery collecting or throwing, music.
- *Travel.* If you will be traveling as part of your sabbatical, study your destination, its history, culture, economics. Find a local newspaper on the Internet. Read some of the literature from that place.
- *Fiction.* Read a series of novels by the same author. Get a copy of *The New York Times Book Review* and discover new fiction.
- *History.* Research a time period that interests you.
- *Faith.* Study extensively in your own or another faith tradition—the desert fathers, mystics, Reformation writers.

Chapter 6

The Dispensable Pastor

Journal: Learning a Different Way of Being a Pastor

September 17, 2001

It has always been clear to me that no one is indispensable. This week it became abundantly clear to me that I am not indispensable. I see this as a good thing.

Last Tuesday, as I was baking bread in the kitchen, I watched on television as an airplane hit the second tower of the World Trade Center. With much of America, I was completely horrified as the morning's events unfolded. As the day passed and I spent too much time watching the same scenes over and over, descriptive words failed me. I read the day's Psalms with the television on as the biblical words fastened onto terrifying images they were never meant to describe.

By the next day words of my own had begun to form. Not words of explanation (there are none) or condemnation or warning, but words of comfort, of searching, of pleading, of being with. They were the words of a sermon for the coming Sunday.

Even as the words formed, I realized I would have nowhere to preach them. I am, I truly recognize for the first time, a preacher without a pulpit. Up until now it has been fine with me not to have to prepare and preach a sermon every week. I have enjoyed writing different kinds of things without the pressure of a weekly deadline. This week, though, I felt a need to be among my church friends, to hear where they were when the sky fell on New York, Washington, and Pennsylvania, to lead us in prayer and in reflecting on the Word of God, and to do what I could to help us know God's peace.

Since that was not a possibility, I went to my new temporary church home at West Cincinnati Presbyterian Church. And it was there it became clear to me I am not indispensable. I was among my church friends. I heard where they were when the sky fell on New York, Washington, and Pennsylvania. We were led in prayer that reflected our worries and thoughts and feelings. And we heard a sermon that brought us God's peace. My own sermon did not have to be preached, and no one was the worse for not having heard it. How strange and warm it felt to hear the word preached, reflecting the feelings of the congregation and the country through the thoughts and words of the particular preacher. I was truly glad to have been there and to worship with my new friends in that place.

Back in my church, Florence Beaujon preached a fabulous sermon (as I knew she would), bringing a true and good word from God's Word. Jerry took notes and even the notes were comforting and uplifting. The choir sang good music; people prayed good prayers. The youth have planned their own prayer service for next Sunday night when they will invite the whole community. I had nothing to do with any of it.

Here's what I learned: No new towers collapsed and my own congregation did not fail or fall because I was not there for the most serious national crisis in recent memory. Of course this is true. I knew it was true before this week. But I did not *know* it to be true in the deepest sense. Pastors—and perhaps most people— think we are so connected to our jobs that things cannot possibly run as smoothly if we are not there to make it so. To learn I was wrong about this was a great relief to my psyche. I believe it will have lasting effects in my work. *I am not responsible to make things run smoothly.* This is the job of all God's people in our particular church, and it is the responsibility of God. Certainly, I am part of that, but only a part, and not an essential one. This gives me the freedom to be who I am apart from my work.

Freedom. I am learning something about my personal freedom during this sabbatical. It seems odd to write this, because I am quite the advocate of personal freedom and responsibility, but I am learning better to differentiate myself from my work. Not being a workaholic (that is, someone who would rather be working than doing anything else), I never thought of myself as having a differentiation problem, but I've come to believe differently. My whole life, I have always done things I enjoy for my employment, and I have never had a job I could leave at the office. Work is a part of who I am, and often I spend my evenings at home engaged in composing a sermon, making pastoral phone calls, writing notes, planning for meetings, and so forth. I tell myself this will free up more time the next day, and it does, but it only frees up more time for more work. When will I make more time for all the other things I love doing in my life? I am not needed nearly as much as part of my mind tells me I am.

Well, I am making more time for those things now. I was baking bread when the towers fell—baking bread on a Tuesday morning. Now that is something. My plan for the rest of that day had been to move from kitchen to office or porch for writing, then to take some black-and-white photographs in the garden. I did make it out to harvest tomatoes and greens from which Jerry and I cooked an interesting supper, then we spent a couple of hours gardening before dark.

What I am learning in my deepest parts is what I already knew in my head: the world of our congregation will keep turning even if I take time for non-work-related things in my life. I need not feel guilty, even when I return to my regular schedule, for living a fuller and more balanced life, for enjoying the time I spend with my husband, for allowing myself to spread into new and exciting areas. I am not making an excuse for laziness; rather, I hope I am learning a rationale for balance.

Following September 11, I seem to be reevaluating my life and its priorities along with many other Americans.

A New Way of Being

It's not only the members of the congregation who sometimes have trouble maintaining the agreed-upon boundaries; pastors may also find it difficult. When crisis occurs, it is hard to stay away for various reasons. Many of those reasons are good ones. We are part of a certain congregational family, and they are part of us. We understandably want to be with them in difficult times. We need their comfort as much as they need ours. With few exceptions, though, we should maintain the boundaries, allowing members and ourselves to grow in different ways through the crisis. Soon enough we will be back together, sharing stories of how we all coped, and learning from the experience of separation.

September 11, 2001 was a wake-up call to many of us. The fact that it happened during my sabbatical made its effect on me particularly strong. Already I was in the mode of reflection and evaluation. The fertile ground of my heart and will had been tilled and was waiting for new seeds to be planted. The seeds that were scattered across our country were not what any of us would have chosen, but they forced us to think about priority, relevance, and importance.

Most pastors do not have such a dramatic national crisis during their leave, but many do come to dramatic, even drastic, realizations and resolve about their work styles and personal life. Whatever has become out of kilter often shows itself in high relief against the backdrop of sabbatical. If we do not recognize and deal with these problems now, will we ever?

Understanding these concepts is important to the health and wholeness of clergy and congregations. We clergy must be able to let go of believing no one can get along without us. We need to help the congregation let go of that belief as well. Rick Herman of Wheat Ridge Ministries says, "[Sabbatical] can be a way to help create a healthier understanding of the pastor (or other church worker's) role in the congregation; i.e., it can help people realize that the ministry of the church is more than the pastor."

Every time we encourage our congregations to think we are essential to their well being, we do them and us a great disservice. Because pastors commonly deal with human needs, some can develop a "need to be needed." This is extremely unhealthy. If such a pattern has occurred, sabbatical can be the time to regain a healthy balance. In other cases, the congregation's needs and expectations may be so overwhelming, the pastor may have difficulty differentiating from those needs. Again, sabbatical can give the distance to restore a healthy relationship.

Steven Reuben, a California rabbi, had been at his congregation for 16 years before taking his first sabbatical. His words were common to the ones I heard from many interviews:

> I remember being excited, high, and thrilled that I had so much time ahead without the congregational responsibilities. For me

it was all travel and play with my wife, which was an amazing treat. I wasn't worried about anything related to work except whether or not they would still try to find me whenever someone died. It was a real sense of personal renewal. There was a deepening sense of my appreciation for how blessed I am, how much I love my work and life, and how important it is to be away from it on a consistent basis so as not to feel trapped by it and resentful.

This is the type of contemplation that ought to characterize spiritual leaders of congregations. Nevertheless, we often don't allow ourselves the luxury of such thought until we have great amounts of time or are faced with some great crisis, whether personal or on a larger scale.

One of the themes emerging from my interviews and from this book is that pastoral leaders who are healthy find they stay longer in their congregations, and congregations with healthy pastors are healthy themselves. Our culture may idolize the workaholic leader, but that leadership style does not best serve the congregation. Balanced leaders make for balanced congregations.

The Lilly Endowment's Jean Smith sees the same correlation. "Pastors tell me that the problems do not go away while they are on sabbatical, but what changes is that they work through these problems in an entirely different way. They return from a time of being away with an entirely new perspective."

Commonly, pastors post-sabbatical remarked that they were so changed by the experience of rest and renewal, they were much more capable of reacting to and working through congregational problems. This was directly related to their time of reflection on the relation between work and self, and how the health of the two are inextricably intertwined. A correctly designed sabbatical will never be so crammed with travel, study, or projects that it does not allow for considerable time just to reflect and to be.

Are we dispensable? Of course. Is this a good thing for us to learn about ourselves? Absolutely. Only then can we have a truly healthy picture of how we relate to our calling.

For Inspiration

Read an inspiring story about a humble leader (for instance, Francis of Assisi, Therese of Lisieux) whose understanding of self was not wrapped up in the needs and expectations of others.

In your journal: Where were you on September 11, 2001? How did that day affect your life, your ministry?

For Contemplation

Make a list of your major accomplishments in the congregation you currently serve. Then make a list of all the other people who helped make those things happen. Let it be a reminder that you do not work alone; God calls and uses many people to do the work.

For Action

Look over your sabbatical plan, including the boundaries you have set for when or if you will be available to the congregation. Resolve now to keep with those boundaries for their sake and for yours.

If you are now in the middle of your sabbatical (or even if you haven't yet begun), spend some of your devotional time rethinking your personal and spiritual priorities. Have they changed? If so, how will your life now reflect the new ones? If not, how true are you being to the priorities you hold dear?

For Further Study

Some books about church organizations assist with understanding congregational change as it relates to the leadership. If part of our sabbatical process is to become better leaders for our congregations in changing times, it may be helpful to recognize the connection between the two concepts.

Markham, Donna J. *Spiritlinking Leadership: Working through Resistance to Organizational Change*. New York: Paulist Press, 1999. Chapter six is about healthy leaders.

Bandy, Thomas G. *Moving Off the Map: A Field Guide to Changing the Congregation*. Nashville: Abingdon Press, 1998. Bandy's second chapter is about church leadership and the need for authenticity among leaders.

Mead, Loren B. *Transforming Congregations for the Future*. Washington, D.C.: The Alban Institute, 1994. See especially the section of chapter 5 that speaks of unhealthy systems.

Chapter 7

Travel in Sabbatical

Journal: The Trip

October 14, 2001

We have just begun the long airplane trip from Glasgow to Amsterdam, to Minneapolis, to Cincinnati, then home. It will give us time to relax and to reflect on the part of our sabbatical journey that is nearly at an end.

Last year, when we began to think about where we would like to go if we were able to take the sabbatical, we settled quickly on Scotland. As Presbyterians who grew up in other denominations, our adopted cultural heritage is traced to that country. In addition, both Jerry and I have always been taken by photographs of the Scottish landscapes.

Now, we have just completed our 15-day visit, and we are full of new experiences and thoughts. I hardly know where to begin.

Probably I should begin with the postponed beginning. We were supposed to fly to Scotland on September 13. The events of September 11 changed that, of course, and we had to scramble to change all our plans. Not only did we have to get new flight arrangements, we needed to call all the bed-and-breakfast establishments where we expected to stay, and see if we could get new accommodations at such a late date.

What I did not expect, as I began to make phone calls to people I'd never met in Scotland, was how solicitous everyone was. They were so caring, and each one asked if we knew anyone who had been affected by the attacks. They told us, to a person, how shocked and horrified they had been as they watched the towers collapse even as we were watching in America. They were glad to make whatever arrangements were needed to reschedule our stay, and not one of them even mentioned that they normally charge a cancellation fee that close to the original arrival date.

We flew into Glasgow on September 19, and found, over the next two weeks, that people were incredibly kind. I believe Scotland would have been a friendly place no matter what, but the timing of our trip made us realize just what an amazing place it is.

Many folks say that travel is an important part of a sabbatical experience, and I have certainly found that to be true in my case. Over the next weeks and months I am sure I will reflect more deeply on this experience, but even at such a close distance I can already see some ways in which I have been affected by it.

For one thing, travel requires flexibility. Oh, I suppose one could choose to be inflexible when traveling, but then the trip would likely be less fun, and certainly would be less interesting. How else would we have taken some side roads to see a "blackhouse" (an ancient-style earthen house with a thatched roof which had been occupied until the late 1960s), which affected us so much by making us imagine the difficult living situation of its residents? We would have missed taking a five-minute ferry ride to the tiny Shetland Island of Bressay, where we had a blast of a day hiking along country roads, leaning into 50-mile-an-hour winds, talking to crofters who were loading some sheep to go the mainland, glimpsing a herd of wild ponies, taking "a pint and a pot" in the local pub, and sharing the harbor with a couple of seals. We would not have taken a ride in the 16-foot wooden skiff of one of our hosts across the loch to climb a hill for a fabulous view of the sea and the peat-covered Isle of Lewis. Jerry would have missed playing golf one morning in the town of Portree, with rented clubs and alongside sheepherders accompanied by their dogs, overlooking the town on one side and the North Sea on the other. We would have missed a poetry reading in a theater attached to John Knox's house in Edinburgh, where the people were delightfully friendly and artsy, and we had a frightful time trying to understand their English, much less the Scots and Gaelic. We would have missed many conversations, fabulous food, hikes through cities and countryside, and even a few nearly perfect photographs. This isn't to say we didn't have a plan. But the flexibility of travel is one of the things that appeals most to us.

Another benefit of travel is how it nearly always reminds us of what is important. It is a truism that families who go camping together find themselves drawn closer. The shared experience of being drenched in a rainstorm or running across a snake is one they can laugh about for years to come. Jerry and I have so many experiences like that from this trip. I suspect we will talk about it as long as we live. Some of the most memorable times are those of the kindness of people.

Our first day in Scotland we landed in Glasgow early in the morning and decided to walk around the city. We explored the university and the shops, and stumbled upon a Church of Scotland that had this sign posted outside: "Until further notice, we will hold two prayer services each day due to the international situation caused by the terrorist attacks in America." We returned to the church for the next service, and found ourselves inside a beautiful old building with two church members and the pastor. He read Psalm 42 and others, and he prayed. He made time and space and silence for us to pray. Our being there, literally in a foreign place, made us realize what is important to us about our own lives and our country. It also brought to the forefront our connection with people of faith around the world. We understood, in a way we could never have felt at home, we were not alone.

Travel is also mind expanding. We have learned so much in such a short time we haven't even begun to assimilate it all. Through castles, museums, churches, and conversations we learned political, social, and religious history. The vast differences in the landscape from one end of Scotland to the other made striking impressions on us. We had heard of the peat-covered Outer Hebrides Islands, but until we walked across the six-foot-deep spongy peat and talked to our gardener/sheep farmer host, we did not realize how the peat itself had shaped a culture. We moved quietly among the Standing Stones of Callanish (somewhat like Stonehenge) and wondered, along with the thousands who had passed that way before us, about the people who had designed and built such a monument, and speculated as to their purpose. We climbed Ben Nevis, rode an overnight ferry to the Shetlands, were serenaded by a 12-year-old player of the Scottish harp beside the fire in the den of her family's guest house, and, yes, we walked part of the Old Course in St. Andrews because it opens as a city park on Sundays. In each of these places, we learned more about the people, land, and culture of Scotland.

It was good for us to be in another country soon after the terrorist attacks. Not only did we experience the healing of warm hospitality, but we were able to hear a European perspective, which is not easily available at home. Both broadcast and print media during our stay had a much more international flavor than our reporting in America. And in our conversations with people we learned different points of view. Our young musician hostess asked if we were from America and wanted to know about the attacks, since they had discussed the situation at her school. I asked her what her teachers had to say. She said, "They said that America came to our aid during the war when we needed help. Now we will help them."

Today we are taking home a planeload of memories and experiences. I believe this travel adventure will help me to be a better pastor.

Travel

Life, especially the spiritual life, is often described as a journey. A metaphor, yes, but also a description of how we learn the art of living. If we stay in one place, either literally or figuratively, we have a truncated view of God's world and the people in it. Travel, for those who are able, exposes the wanderer to new scenes, new conversations, new settings. This enlarging of self cannot be obtained from watching the Travel Network; it must be experienced by going to another place.

Nearly every clergyperson I interviewed for this book had travel as a component of sabbatical. Some went overseas, while others stayed closer to home. All who traveled believed their sabbatical experience had been richer because of those experiences. And each one's experiences were different from those of others. Travel also helps the pastor disengage from the parish: When you're in Germany no one will call you for advice or to find out where the key to the janitor's closet is.

Jim Antal, for example, on sabbatical from his pastorate in Ohio, drove to Montana for a three-week study time with a university professor. They explored theological ideas, and the possibility of writing a book together at some future time. On the other hand, Holly McKissick went with her husband and children to France and Italy for several weeks. There she studied sacred spaces, and spent time experiencing new cultures with her family. Jeff Hosmer, a pastor in Cincinnati, spent several weeks at a seminary just a couple of hours from home working on his Doctor of Ministry project.

It may seem trite to say that travel is important because of the experience, but it is true. Now, months after our trip, we are often reminded of someone we met or of someplace we walked. Even after several washings, I can still smell the distinctive smoke when I put on the sweater I was wearing the day we visited the blackhouse with its constant fire of dried peat. Nearly every time we cook salmon we remember the salmon and scallops cooked for us the first night we stayed in a home on the Isle of Lewis, creatures that had just been harvested from the sea right outside the door. When international conflicts flare, we wonder what our new acquaintances in Scotland would have to say. We have been changed by that place.

Not everyone, of course, will be able to or even want to travel to some place far away during a sabbatical. Nevertheless, getting away from home, even if it's not a great distance, has tremendous advantages for the rest and renewal you need and want. I spent only five of my 15 weeks away from home, and two of those weeks were taken up with courses. The other three, though (in distant Scotland and at Red River Gorge just a couple of hours from home), were in some ways absolutely key to the sabbatical experience.

I am not sure we grow more when we are away from home, but I do think we may grow differently. We can become so caught up in the routines of daily chores and schedules, even on sabbatical, that we need a new environment in which to set our minds working and to put our minds at rest. New places open up new experiences, new relationships, and new risks. We are forced to act outside our normal environment.

If you are on a budget, you may have to do a little research to find an inexpensive place to visit. Many monasteries and convents take in travelers for extended stays at very reasonable cost. Most of them offer meals and a spartan, though comfortable, living area. Sometimes they even have "hermitages" on their properties, places where you can be in seclusion for rest or study. Depending on your needs or desires, you will want to see which ones offer meals only in community, expect attendance at worship services, or don't allow guests at worship services. Communicate all your questions to the religious house ahead of time to make sure what they offer fits your needs.

Another possibility for the budget-minded sabbatical traveler is a home exchange. Your judicatory may have a list of clergy who are willing to trade homes for a week, a month, or more. Sometimes this involves offering pastoral services in the new location, and sometimes not. Again, you will want to be sure of expectations before you go.

Perhaps a friend of yours, or a member of your congregation, has a vacation home that is not always used. They might be glad to have someone occupy it for a time, paying the utilities and keeping it clean. The same could be true for friends or family who live somewhere else and could use a house sitter while they are away for an extended trip. Does someone you know in another place have a garage apartment behind the house? Would they be willing to rent it to you inexpensively for a month?

If you are willing to do some work of a different sort in your sabbatical, you may want to explore the idea of a short-term mission project. For very little expense, you can travel to a mission outpost and exchange your labor for meals and a place to sleep.

Many judicatories have camps and conference centers that

offer inexpensive rates for clergy and their families, for short or long stays. If yours does not, check with other denominations about what they may have available.

Whatever you decide to do, be sure you think about the kind of place that will bring you rest and renewal. Jerry and I, for example, are not really big-city people. We like visiting cities for a few days, but we truly draw our energy from countryside and nature. Knowing that about ourselves, we focused our Scotland trip on the sparsely populated Highlands and islands, planning in significant time for hiking and other outdoor activities. We visited Glasgow, Edinburgh, and St. Andrews, but the bulk of our time was spent in the mountains and hiking through the country or small towns. We packed very lightly and carried our clothing in backpacks to make ourselves more mobile.

If you, on the other hand, serve a rural parish but miss city life, see if you can find an inexpensive place to stay in New York, London, Tokyo, or San Francisco. This may take a little research, but it will be well worth it.

If you need to be on the water for renewal, think of a family member with a lake cottage, or travel to the ocean in the off-season when it is less expensive. Spend a couple of weeks camping by a trout stream, or canoeing the boundary waters of Canada.

If you are up for it, camping and backpacking are extremely inexpensive ways to travel, and the fresh air and physical activity will probably be a huge change from your usual world. Not ready to set up a tent in the rain? You can always rent a camper and take a cross-country trip, or find one spot to settle in for a few weeks.

Whatever you decide to do, and wherever you decide to go, let it be primarily a place where you believe you will be renewed. Renewal is often a function of many things: state of mind; activity or inactivity; physical exercise and rest. Renewal may also be a function of place. Find a good place where you can put together the pieces of your sabbatical. If you're not open to growth and change, a sabbatical is probably not the right move for you just now. On the other hand, if you are open to the leading of God's Spirit, wherever that may take you, pick up a travel book and start dreaming.

For Inspiration

Go to a travel agency or to the travel section of your local library. Pick up brochures or books of any places that look interesting, whether near home or across the globe. Investigate different types of travel, from organized tours to adventure travel to renting a single place to put down roots for a few weeks. Take them home and daydream.

Write a journal entry about a special place. Why is it meaningful to you?

For Contemplation

What is it you want from your travel experiences? Do you want to experience another culture or visit family you haven't seen in years? Have you always wanted to visit the land of your heritage? Do you want to stretch your physical limits, or explore a place rich in history? Do you want to spend time in nature, or walking the streets of an ancient city? Is the thought of spending time in a spiritual retreat center appealing? What will renew you? What will renew your family relationships?

For Action

1. Will you be traveling alone or with a spouse or other family? Sit down with all involved and list your interests in regards to travel, along with any special needs (e.g., dietary or physical limitations). Begin a list of places you might want to go. Keep it on the refrigerator or some other location where you will see it often, so you can add to it when new thoughts occur.
2. Go back to your ideas about funding, and see how your travel plans fit. Have you considered some of the ideas in this chapter for less expensive ways to travel? Don't give up the chance of travel, even if it means scaling back some of your plans.

For Further Study

Here are some books that may inspire your travel plans if you are interested in spiritual retreat:

Hughes, Colonel James J. (Ret.) and Victoria D. Hughes, eds. *Overnight or Short Stay at Religious Houses around the World.* Bloomfield, N.J.: Hugen Press, 1995.

Jones, Timothy. *A Place for God: A Guide to Spiritual Retreats and Retreat Centers.* New York: Image Books, 2000.

Though this next book is about taking groups on mission trips, it has helpful information for those taking such trips alone. It can be ordered from the Presbyterian Church's Distribution Service, at 1-800-524-2612:

Vial, Debby D. *When God's People Travel Together: A Trip Leader's Planning Manual.* Louisville: The Presbyterian Church (USA), 1999.

Finally, here is a short list of books by people who have amazing stories to tell about travel:

Fisher, M. F. K. *The Gastronomical Me.* San Francisco: Northpoint Press, 1989.

Mayes, Frances. *Under the Tuscan Sun: At Home in Italy.* New York: Broadway Books, 1997.

Neale, Tom. *All in the Same Boat.* Camden, Me.: International Marine, 1997.

The Travelers' Tales Series, published by Travelers' Tales, Inc. (Each book contains essays about a particular place or type of travel; see www.travelerstales.com for more information.)

Chapter 8

Being Away

Journal: Day by Day

October 24, 2001

As time goes on, I find it easier to stay away from the church and its needs. I hear about them through Jerry and am interested in what goes on there, but more as a casual observer or an occasional guest rather than as the pastor.

I have been on sabbatical now for about two-and-a-half months and I have a month left. The passing of time in its gentle way leads me to new thoughts and conclusions about my life and my work.

First, I find myself increasingly committed to staying at this church, but drastically aware that some things must change. Whereas I previously wondered if I would be able to remain here at all, the time away has indeed renewed my call to this particular place. At this point in time I do not see going anywhere else for some time. Not only are the people and the place dear to me, I simply don't feel as though we have accomplished all we have been called to do together.

On the other hand, I have also become deeply committed to change. As a matter of fact, without change, I am certain I will not be able to stay here. Some of the changes are mine to make; some are changes that need to take place in the congregation.

Specifically, I must change old habits of overwork. Because I enjoy doing new things, and because in a church, as in many jobs, there is always something else needing to be done, I see a future of simply working myself into stress-related illnesses again, until I am forced to take a different kind of sabbatical—the kind that comes between jobs. I will have to retrain myself to work a shorter week, and retrain the congregation to expect fewer hours from me, even if it means some things don't get done.

Among many things I have learned about myself during the last couple of months is that I need to develop more outside interests. I love a wide variety of activities and projects, and have delighted in this time of writing, taking photographs, gardening, and so forth. I don't want to let these activities go because they make me a more interesting and balanced person. I will use those extra hours to keep up with my other interests. I feel I owe these changes, not only to myself and my congregation, but also to the next pastor, whenever and whoever that may be. No one needs to follow a pastor who worked too much.

Other than needing to make some deep changes in my work habits, the second major conclusion I have reached has to do with my marriage and family. Jerry and I have always been close, but the time we've shared during this sabbatical has been delightful. We have worked like this before, sharing an office, but never to this extent. Sometimes we go out to lunch together, we take a break to read the mail, we cook together most evenings. We have not tired of one another's company nor felt a great need to be alone. I have had a glimpse of our retirement years and they are looking pretty darned good.

I've also had more time to connect with my parents, though they live several states away, and with my stepdaughters, also out of state. There is something about the fewer constraints of pressing need that has allowed me to make those connections more easily. This, too, is something I don't want to lose when I go back to my usual work.

I don't want to forget how much fun it is to eat lunch with Jerry or to be home in time to cook supper with him. I don't want to be distracted from the importance of family by the importance of work.

All in all, I have found this time of contemplation to be quite fruitful. As I reflect on the things that are important to me, the list has not changed, nor the priorities of the items on the list. What has changed, though, is the realization of my desire to be more balanced. "Balance" is a word I have used so many times in this journal, as it is something I am striving to reassert. Balance is important in the life of faith, and the achieving of it should perhaps be listed among the spiritual disciplines. It has been the most essential accomplishment of my sabbatical.

A Balanced Life

Probably every person who goes on sabbatical will take away learnings and developments that are unique. However, there is some wisdom that surfaces commonly across different experiences.

Many realize how unbalanced their lives have become once some balance is restored. Their relief is so tangible they vow never to return to their old ways of being. Maintaining the equilibrium is difficult, though. No matter how much we try, old habits of working creep in. It takes determination and vigilance to keep a steady course among all that is important to us.

Disconnecting may be as hard for the pastor as for the congregation. Again, it is helpful to set firm boundaries in the sabbatical policy and keep to them. Some pastors, while away, sent in monthly newsletter articles or reports to be read at worship. Others found it more helpful to have absolutely no contact.

While we are away from our congregations, there are certain disciplines that are helpful in achieving whatever balance we may have lost.

- Worship. Regular worship at a place other than your own is important. You may wish to find a place to put down temporary roots and attend worship there regularly, or you may find it more helpful to your spiritual life to worship somewhere different each week. Enjoy the very act of not having to prepare or lead worship. Let God's presence speak to you.
- Pray. Explore the time you have been given to reestablish your prayer life.
- De-complicate. Remember that now you have the chance to do what you are always wanting to do: simplify your life. You probably don't have to be anywhere at any certain time most days. Enjoy that lack of structure and allow yourself to be spontaneous.
- Observe. Pay attention to the rhythms of life and to the people you love. Notice what is important to you. Act on those things.

So many people I interviewed mentioned how their sabbatical helped them become more involved with their spouse or family. It is common knowledge that the family life of pastors often suffers because of strange hours and time demands. Sabbatical turns that world of meetings and weekend sermon preparations around so that there is now the time we imagine other people have with their families.

Occasionally, family problems can surface during a sabbatical. Not unlike when a person retires or is between jobs, a spouse who is suddenly around all the time may change the family dynamics. Issues of "turf" or "too much togetherness" may be problematic. Or some difficulty that has been hidden from view because of the hectic lives family members lead may now appear. If so, family counseling may prove to be an important part of your sabbatical.

Whether your clergy leave involves family or not, it should definitely give you the time to reorganize your priorities if necessary. Achieving balance in our relationships and in our work is something many of us neglect much of the time. There will never be a better time than this.

For Inspiration

Write a journal entry about balanced living. When have you seen it or lived it? What steps do you need to take in order to have more equilibrium in your life?

For Contemplation

If you have not done so recently, make a list of the most important people and values in your life. How are they reflected or neglected in the way you live? How might a sabbatical restore some balance to the equation that is your daily living?

For Action

If you have a spouse and/or children, make sure they are involved in your sabbatical planning. Remember that whatever you do will affect them. How much togetherness or separate time will your plans require?

For Further Study

Some books about living the life of faith:

Bass, Dorothy C., ed. *Practicing Our Faith: A Way of Life for a Searching People*. San Francisco: Jossey-Bass, 1998.
Gallagher, Nora. *Things Seen and Unseen: A Year Lived in Faith*. New York: Vintage Books, 1999.
Livingston, Patricia H. *This Blessed Mess*. Notre Dame, Ind.: Sorin Books, 2001.

If you are interested in living a simpler life, whatever that may mean to you, check out a book on that subject, such as *The Simple*

Living Guide: A Sourcebook for Less Stressful, More Joyful Living, by Janet Luhrs (New York: Broadway Books, 1997).

Chapter 9

In the Midst of Sabbath

Journal: Learning Sabbath

November 7, 2001

The camera has taught me how better to experience sabbath. Today is not a Sunday, the Sabbath day of most Christians, but it doesn't matter. As a pastor, Sunday is rarely my Sabbath anyway. Jerry and I are in the Red River Gorge in Kentucky for a week of rest. This morning I dropped him off at a golf course and I went hiking with my camera. I returned to a waterfall we had seen on Sunday afternoon, and spent a couple of hours just looking at it through the lens of my camera.

With no one else around, I felt free to take my time. I was not obstructing anybody's view, and no one was waiting for me.

I stopped at the place on the path where Jerry and I had first seen the falls a few days earlier. I took a few quick shots. I followed the path we had taken, crossing the streambed on rocks above the falls. This time I stopped and turned back to look at the rocks I'd just crossed. In the filtered light of the deep woods, they seemed almost to emit their own moist, slick light, covered as they were with mosses and mold. I changed the lens on my camera and knelt down to photograph the rocks.

When I stood I was looking down over the edge of the falls, a new perspective. More photos. Then I continued walking down the far side of the falling stream, looking for interesting frames and light. It's all about light, I thought.

In August, when I took my photography course, the learning curve for me had been very steep. I'd feared I would be the only one in my class who didn't know how to use all the doohickeys on my new camera. As it turned out, everyone in my introductory class to black-and-white photography was similarly inexperienced. Lisa, our instructor, was quite patient as she taught us the beginnings of both the technique and art of photography during our weeklong course. The first day was difficult as we learned about f-stops, shutter speeds, and the zone system. We took field trips on subsequent days to a lighthouse, a boatyard, an old fort, a lobster pound, an historic village. Every day I learned a little more about my camera, composition, artistry, and light.

It's all about light, I thought again today, always and especially light. I found myself drawn to ripples in the stream, leaves hanging overhead, the aerated water tumbling over the rocks, all because of how they differently reflected and played with the light. It's as though I'd learned to see differently through and because of the camera.

I've always been such a left-brained person. Reason and deliberate action are what move me. But this camera thing is changing me. It's almost as though (I know this sounds crazy) I can feel my brain switching sides, firing in new places and in different ways. I have found myself evolving, expanding my thought as I compose a photograph. Not consciously, really, but truly nevertheless.

As I photographed the falls earlier today, I had the same experience I have had many times while taking pictures during this sabbatical. Somewhere in the process I realized my breathing had slowed. I had calmed, almost as if I were involved in contemplative, meditative prayer. Somewhere (I think maybe it was when I was kneeling to look at the rocks) my photography did become a sort of prayer. I became intensely aware of the light and of the wonder of creation. I became intensely aware of God's presence. It is not as though I vocalized this, even internally; it just was. After that, I was moving differently, in a changed state of mind, toward some undefined goal that may have been just a fuller sense of God.

Strange, isn't it, that a minister would feel closer to God taking a few pictures? I first experienced this at the fort during my photography class. My classmates came looking for me because I had completely lost track of the time. I would have guessed I had been gone from them about 15 minutes; it had been over two hours. The different state of mind I'd entered had taken me out of my normal sense of time. I was embarrassed (being a person always aware of the time), but I could tell something new was happening to me. The creative experience I'd sought had come to me when I wasn't aware of it. As I rode in the car to the next assignment, I silently noted how I felt and what I was thinking. It was as though God's spirit was finding a new access to my mind.

I have since learned I don't have to be alone to experience this renewal. Sometimes when Jerry and I are out together, we share the camera, pointing out possible photos to each other, suggesting exposures and stops, using a minimum of words but feeling a strong connection with what we are doing, with the beauty of the surroundings, and with one another. It has happened here in the gorge, at home in our garden, even taking architectural photos. In our slowing down to see, we become more closely related to each other and to God.

So today's experience was not the first of its kind for me, but I realize it's something I want to repeat often. This altered consciousness, this altered sense of time, is, I believe, one of the essences of sabbath. Sabbath seems to be largely about time and our reintroduction to God's time, which stands in stark relief to our own. God's sabbath set aside a whole day for remembering, for rest, for reconnecting with God and people, and for worship. My sabbath in Red River Gorge has been all of those things in abundance. I have consciously remembered and reflected on the goodness of God. I have slept plenty and rested in the ways that are most meaningful for me. I have read my Bible, I've seen God in every place I've been, and I've enjoyed Jerry's company immensely. I have even worshiped through the lens of my camera.

When I go away after taking photographs, I find I still see the world differently, even when my camera is no longer with me. This new sense lasts for a while, then starts to fade. In my mind soon after a photo session, I frame a picture of the sky through the maple tree outside our bedroom window; I walk across the yard to see the raspberry blossoms close-up; I imagine a stop-frame of children I see playing hopscotch on the sidewalk; I notice how the shape of a familiar building stands in contrast to the clouds passing over it. When several days have passed after my last taking of pictures, I see these things less often. When several weeks have passed, I see them rarely or not at all. But all it takes is one good photo session to renew my special sight.

I think this is also true with our practice of spiritual disciplines, especially sabbath observance. When I take a true sabbath, one which takes me away from seeing life simply in terms of my labor and focuses my sight on God and other people, I find that I carry that vision, that new way of seeing, back into my ordinary living. True sabbath can come to me through gardening, hiking, sailing, and yes, worship. In the times when I am most open to the moving of God's spirit, whether consciously or unconsciously, I am changed by an awareness of the holy, the separate. I am moved to think outside the bounds of my work, to forget my lists and my desk, and to lose myself in the moment of rest and new awareness. I hope I will somehow learn how to carry this back to my post-sabbatical life, so I may remember.

Sabbath and Sabbatical

It may sound a little obvious that the concept of *sabbatical* comes from the word *sabbath*. *Sabbath* is a word with many variations of meaning, not least of which is ceasing from work. As Marva Dawn says, there is (or should be) a rhythm of moving back and forth between work and rest. The problem is, we tend to glorify the working, but rarely do we allow ourselves and others to glorify the resting.[1] Nowhere is this more true than among clergy, who like to brag about how many hours we work in a week. Few of us feel comfortable telling others how rested we feel after a good night's sleep. Instead, we tell the stories of how we were awakened in the night by an emergency call, went to the hospital, and have had a full day of appointments since then. We tell about the number of workdays in a row without a day off, but are embarrassed to admit how much we enjoyed a day in the woods, or at the zoo, or reading a novel in the hammock.

Time is valued in our culture, but not in itself. Time is often seen as something to be filled up, blank spaces on the daily planner waiting for appointments. Our importance as people is often judged by how full our time is, and how efficiently we schedule it. Rarely do we think of time as a discipline, a way to connect with God. According to Wayne Muller, "The Sabbath is a revolutionary invitation to consider that the fruits of our labor may be found in the restful and unhurried harvest of time. In time, we can taste the sweetness of peace, serenity, well-being, and delight."[2]

Marjorie Thompson, speaking to the 2002 triennial meeting of the National Association of Presbyterian Clergywomen on the topic of time and sabbath rest, encouraged pastors to remember that the biblical concept of sabbath is not just rest for rest's sake, but rest in order to experience and enjoy more fully both God and the things God has made. The early church fathers, says Thompson, understood the concept of "holy leisure." They defined work as "non-leisure," rather than leisure as "non-work," the way we usually think of things. To rest in God is to critique a culture (even the culture of the western church) preoccupied with work. According to Thompson, leisure is not given to us for the purpose of making us work more efficiently. On the other hand, the more we find ourselves capable of giving to God for enjoyment and rest, the more we may find ourselves able to spend our time of labor wisely.

Several thinkers share this concept. Marva Dawn also points out that "a day especially set aside for worship teaches us to carry the spirit of worship into our work. Furthermore, to give ourselves a day's break from emotional and intellectual problems enables us to come back to them with fresh perspectives, creative insights, and renewed spirits."[3]

What is it that brings you "fresh perspective, creative insights, and a renewed spirit"? Can you remember the last time that you had a true sabbath—a day of rest that was so renewing it changed you? Can you remember one in which you left all your work behind and did something for no other purpose than to renew your soul?

For me, nearly any outdoors activity is renewing. I love to hike, garden, sail. I also am blessed to live in a place where the open outdoors is literally right outside my door. Even so, I am embarrassed to realize how little I take advantage of the things I love, because there is always some work to be done.

When we fail to renew our sense of time in the presence of God, we find ourselves overwhelmed by the demands on our time. It is as though our bucketful of time and energy has been turned upside down and the last drops are being drained out of it. Sabbath, and sabbatical, are about keeping the bucket balanced between what is being poured in and what is being poured out.

When was the last time you spent a rainy day reading a novel, or a sunny day visiting a museum? When was the last time you visited with an old friend for several hours, not just for a quick lunch between appointments? When was the last time you took a real, honest-to-goodness day off and did nothing but play?

As you plan your sabbatical, I encourage you to imagine what will bring you pleasure and take you away from your work. What will bring you closer to God and refill your empty bucket? What will turn you around and send you renewed back to the work to which you have been called?

Michael Mather, who spent the first part of his sabbatical with his family living in India, then staying at Ghost Ranch Conference Center in New Mexico and traveling across the United States, says his spiritual life was greatly affected by his sabbatical time:

> I think of moments such as standing in front of the Taj Mahal, walking through the largest slum in Asia, walking the streets of Calcutta, climbing up to Chimney Rock every weekday morning for the three months at Ghost Ranch, hiking at Yosemite. . . . Also, while we were in India, we were utterly and completely dependent upon the generosity of strangers. The hospitality of the people we encountered was the most extravagant I have ever experienced. After the sabbatical I think my spiritual life

was most enriched by seeing our place here through the eyes of my experiences in these other places. By that I mean to say that it gave me a great deal of hope in dealing with the struggles people have in this place. I think that upon my return I feel more of a sense of perspective that has greatly enriched my spiritual life.

And that is at least part of the meaning of sabbath.

For Inspiration

In earlier chapters I suggested you imagine the things that would bring you renewal. Why not write a journal entry about one of them? How has it taught you to observe the biblical concept of sabbath? Or, write an entry about what you think sabbath is and how it is present or lacking in your life.

For Contemplation

For me, the photographic seminar was the "release" I needed from some usual ways of thinking and behaving. It moved me much farther into the sabbatical experience than I had previously been. Now photography is something I will always have, unless I am careless and do not practice it. It allows me a "mini-sabbatical" on a Friday afternoon or Tuesday morning, for renewal. Can you imagine what activity might be a similar release for you? It should be something that brings you joy and rest, and brings you more fully into the presence of God.

For Action

List a few creative, restful activities you have always wanted to do, or used to do but no longer make time for. Don't be restricted by time, place, or money when making your list. Order your selections top to bottom. If you were able to gain that new skill, attitude, or experience, how do you think it would change you? Now start to think about where you could go to gain the experience for one of the top items on your list.

Remember: you don't have to wait to take a sabbatical to do this. What things in your life can you change now? What new activity can you learn, or what old one can you rekindle? How will you make time for it?

For Further Study

In addition to the books footnoted, try these:

Thibodeaux, Mark E., S.J. *Armchair Mystic: Easing into Contemplative Prayer.* Cincinnati: St. Anthony Messenger Press, 2001.
Thompson, Marjorie J. *Soul Feast: An Invitation to the Christian Spiritual Life.* Louisville: Westminster John Knox, 1995.
Bass, Dorothy C. *Receiving the Day: Christian Practices for Opening the Gift of Time.* San Francisco: Jossey-Bass, 2000.
Job, Rueben P., and Norman Shawchuck. *A Guide to Prayer for All God's People.* Nashville: Upper Room Books, 1991.
Stairs, Jean. *Listening for the Soul: Pastoral Care and Spiritual Direction.* Minneapolis: Fortress Press, 2000. Especially important for this topic is chapter four about the need for pastoral care-givers to maintain their own spiritual practices.

Chapter 10

Preparing to Reenter

Journal: Almost Over

November 12, 2001

One week from today I will be back at the church. My sabbatical is winding down and I am experiencing the wonder of ending. It feels a little like the last week of summer vacation when I was in school: I know I'll miss the freedom, but it will be good to be back. I'll get to see my friends again, sit at my familiar desk, look around to see what has changed and what has stayed the same.

Certainly one thing that has changed is my outlook. I feel rested, renewed, and ready.

I am ready to return, I think. I have missed my friends at church, even the folks who drive me a little crazy sometimes. I worry, still, about our congregation and where it is headed for the long term, but I worry less than I did. I am more convinced now that the future of the congregation is in God's hands and not in mine. I am full of energy and ideas, but also more aware of my limitations.

Even so, I am experiencing grief at ending the sabbatical. I know my writing will suffer and my heart will be at home, at Red River Gorge, taking pictures, gardening. If I had my druthers I'd certainly keep doing this for a while. I love writing, even the research part. And I love the freedom I have had to choose how I will spend each day. It has been fabulous, without a doubt.

I have dreamed (*bad* dreams) about work nearly every night for the last week. I suppose that should tell me something. The anticipation of returning has seeped into my subconscious. In some of my dreams I feel caught, almost as in a trap, in an inability of the church and me to change.

I wonder sometimes about my need for change and feelings of restlessness. What is their origin? I have recently read several articles that refer to midlife and the changes in attitude that often accompany it. The thing is, though, I have always felt this way. Never have I felt "settled in" and comfortable in any work that continues on in the same way year after year. I love new challenges, creative endeavors, getting to know new people, making new memories.

Sometimes this puts me at odds with the church. Long-term pastorates often become soothing for pastor and congregation because people become used to each other, like in a long marriage. They no longer challenge each other to do new things, to listen for the call of God to act out their faith in new ways. The dance we began 10 years ago as we excitedly learned how to adjust to each other's peculiarities has now sometimes become a shuffle in which we move together, using the same old rhythms and the same old steps, across the dance floor in choreographed, familiar ways. Familiarity can be good and even helpful as we become comfortable with each other and continually learn more about one another's gifts and needs. However, it can also become an excuse for listlessness, requiring neither much thought nor much energy and generating little excitement.

My renewed commitment and call to stay in this church require me to find new sources of energy and freshness. I have come to terms with the belief that some of those sources necessarily will come from outside the church. Now that the sabbatical is nearly over, I hope I will be able to continue scheduling time for those activities. It is hard to imagine spending an hour taking pictures when I could be at the nursing home or hospital or office. The old me would have said "when I *should* be" at those places. The new me is more accepting of my personal needs and more willing to allow their expression in my life and in my work. My calling to be pastor at this church does not mean that I am not also called to be a person in my own right, a child of God with much to give and receive outside the structure of the congregation. And I have finally come to the realization that I will be a better pastor when my own creative needs are met. I have become, I hope, a better preacher, a more attentive pastor, even more of an idea person.

And so, as I wind down the last week of sabbatical, I am starting to pack up my books and papers to go back to the office. In the same cartons I am packing my new energy, ideas, and resolve.

Winding Down

If you are typical, your last weeks of sabbatical will run the gamut of emotion, from grief to anticipation. Assuming your leave has brought you renewal, it is completely natural to grieve its passing. Have you had more time with your family, more time to think and study, more time for rest and creativity? It is difficult to give up those things.

On the other hand, these last weeks are the right time to set your mind and heart ahead, to imagine a different and renewed parish, to dream about change amid familiarity, to refocus your vision.

After all, the sabbatical has not been only about you. It has been about and for both you and the congregation. While you and your renewal have been your focus over the last weeks and months, now your focus needs to shift back to include the congregation in your renewal plans and ideas.

Think about what you have learned during your leave. What have been the most important concepts, ideas, values? This is the time to imagine how to integrate them into your work and share them with your congregation.

Imagine your first time back in the pulpit. What type of sermon will you preach? Will it be just like the sermons you have always preached, or will your listeners know you have been renewed by listening to you? What will you say to express your feelings upon returning to them?

Imagine your first meeting with the governing board. If you plan the agenda, how will it reflect what you have learned? What dreams for the future of the congregation will you express?

Imagine a setting where you will talk with the entire congregation about your sabbatical. What will be the highlights of what you share with them? How will they begin to learn your dreams for the future? How will you show your excitement for the future?

If, when you return to the congregation, you say the same things you did when you left, they will wonder why in the world they invested time and money for your sabbatical when you didn't seem to change any, or didn't seem to learn or grow in any way that would be helpful for them. If you learned anything, or grew at all, your growth should be reflected to them immediately so they can rejoice with you and begin to absorb some of your new energy and ideas. It is as if a new pastor has come to them in the body of the old one they already know and love. In this best of two worlds, the familiarity of the old leads all of you more quickly into the excitement of the new. You have new-fashioned dance steps to show them, but you and they already know how to move together.

It's possible, of course, that you may also find some difficulties when you return to the congregation. There will be more about that in the next chapter. For now, though, be aware that there may be resistance to change or resentment at your long absence.

Plan for this to be a time of newness and familiarity, of renewing relationships and dreaming together about the future. Enjoy your last weeks of sabbatical, and get ready for an exciting ride when you return.

For Inspiration

Make a journal entry recording your thoughts and feelings about this renewal time coming to an end. How has it been for you in the past when you were making transitions? Are changes easy or difficult for you? What joys or problems do you anticipate upon returning?

For Contemplation

Read Genesis 1–2. What new things is God still doing in your congregation and in you?

For Action

1. Make a plan for returning, so it is not simply something that just happens. Whom will you visit? What will your first sermon or public meeting be like? What emotions and thoughts do you want to convey?
2. Write a draft of a newsletter article about your sabbatical.
3. Plan your first governing board meeting. How will you inspire the leaders of the congregation to think in new ways?

For Further Study

Craig, Robert H., and Robert C. Worley. *Dry Bones Live: Helping Congregations Discover New Life*. Louisville: Westminster/John Knox, 1992.

Chapter 11

Returning from Sabbatical

Journal: The First Month Back

December 26, 2001

I don't know what I was thinking when I decided to return to work the week of Thanksgiving! It has been such a busy, up-and-down month, I am just now finding time to write about it.

I thought if I went back the Monday before Thanksgiving, I'd have a short first week and be able to slip into the "work mode" a bit at a time. Instead, the short week was hardly enough time to get back in the swing before we entertained a dozen friends on Thanksgiving Day, not to mention added preparations for my first Sunday back from sabbatical.

The "Welcome Back" party that Sunday was delightful. Great church food was accompanied by seeing all my friends again for the first time in months. It truly was a good homecoming. The fun was complicated, though, by my ambitious ideas for the worship service.

It was Christ the King Sunday, and I used the epistle text to speak of darkness and light, illustrated by slides of some of my black-and-white photographs from the sabbatical, which showed the play of light, especially in dark places. The idea came from my very observant photography instructor in Maine, who noticed this recurring theme in my photographs long before I would have.

This "photographic sermon" was the first visible sign to the church of the results of my sabbatical. However, I spent way too many hours that week selecting and preparing slides and timing the presentation to go along with the sermon. The result was fine, but it put me behind in my work and it took me a long time to catch up.

Then, of course, came Advent with all its extra preparations and visiting all the shut-ins. This was an important reconnection for me, because I had been very concerned about them while I was away, and they were interested to hear what I had done. These were happy reunions, and I took my time with them. There were also projects I'd had time to think about and plan for during my sabbatical, and in my overactive zeal I wanted to start some of them right away. Big mistake.

My personal Advent and Christmas preparations suffered. I don't just mean the putting up of the tree and the baking of cookies (we were late getting to the former and the latter never happened), but the preparations I needed to make in my own heart. Advent is always a busy time, but this year was the most harried for me since my first year of ministry. I tried to make time for my own spiritual needs, but after the first few days, they fell near the bottom of the list. I have been able to maintain a somewhat regular schedule of private devotions, but those daily times became shorter as the month went on, and more disconnected from my practice of ministry and from my life.

There is good news in being back, though. Things went smoothly (actually, better than smoothly) at the church during my absence. People seem genuinely happy to have me back, but also genuinely glad we all had this interesting time away from each other. As far as I know, no major conflicts erupted during the few months I was gone, and none have leapt out since my return.

I am a little tired, but not in the least disheartened. There is a big difference in the tiredness I have now and what I experienced before the sabbatical.

I am taking off the week between Christmas and New Year's Day and have determined to use some of the time to plan the next month a little more carefully and realistically. Here are some of my needs:

- *I need to control my work hours.* Though I thought about this a good deal during my sabbatical, it has been very difficult to implement changes during Advent. I believe now my timing was a mistake, but I wonder if it would have been unrealistic to scale back work hours when returning from a sabbatical at any time of the year. Perhaps I should have expected to hit the ground running for a little while, and planned for that. I have had little time with Jerry this month, and I have missed that greatly. My participation in the enjoyment of our favorite season has been minimal.

- *I need to make time for my spiritual life.* As I mentioned, I have been relatively regular, but that is about all that can be said. After experiencing significant spiritual renewal during my sabbatical, this loss has been particularly painful and unexpected. In the months I was on a different schedule, it's not as though I spent an unusually long time with my devotional life. I suspect the difference I felt then was that the things which were waiting for me to do were not calling as loudly to me as my regular work responsibilities do. Those responsibilities again seem to compete with the voice of God when I sit to read or pray. I have trouble concentrating on what I'm reading because my mind travels to the piles on my desk or the calls to be made.

- *I need to make time for thinking and planning.* This item is related to the one above. When my "to-do" list is long, as it has been all this past month, I find it difficult to carve out necessary planning time. Yet I know that when I am thinking and planning I am a better pastor. Planning allows me time and space to be more creative in my work.
- *I need to make more personal time for creative endeavors.* This time is separate from the creative thinking I need to do for my job, but is not unrelated. In the past month I have not taken a single photograph, nor written anything beyond my sermons and Bible studies. I can almost feel my creativity drying up as it goes unused. This is something I absolutely must not let go after so recently rediscovering its importance to me.
- *I need to remember the sabbath.* Again, all of these needs are interconnected. And all of them have to do with my use of time.

One thing I did right was to plan this week of vacation. It comes after a normally busy season and after a month back at the church. It comes at just the right time. I have been back just long enough to see (I hope) what I am doing wrong, but not long enough to have been completely overwhelmed by or entrenched in bad patterns. If I use this week wisely, again affirming my reasonable needs and determining how to make room for them in my crowded life, I should be able to reestablish balance. I am quite optimistic about doing this.

Reentry

When I spoke to Richard Bruesehoff, co-author of *Clergy Renewal*, about my difficulties in the first month back, he told me this was a huge problem for nearly all the clergy with whom he had spoken. After my own experience, and since interviewing a number of clergy on the topic, I have reached the same conclusion. Perhaps a difficult reentry from an extended leave is almost inevitable.

Anyone who has been away from the office for several months can hardly expect to find a clean desk and calendar upon returning. No matter how expert and professional the staff members have been in your absence, there will be people waiting to see you when you return. Some types of work tend to pile up. Most likely, you will want to jump right in and tackle new projects, using all your newfound energy and enthusiasm. My advice: Go slowly and be cautious. You don't want to use up all that energy and enthusiasm in the first six weeks. You don't want to put yourself right back to where you were before you started.

Perhaps a wise approach the first month or two is this: Expect to be a little overwhelmed and plan accordingly. Don't schedule lots of new projects to begin. Use the first month to settle back in to work; reacquaint yourself with the people, the office, and your main responsibilities; schedule sabbath time; and don't forget the renewing activities of your leave. If you can, plan a week or a few days off sometime soon after the first month or two, and use them to regroup, reevaluate, and renew.

One rabbi spoke of how much he and his wife had enjoyed the extended time together during his four-month sabbatical. After returning to work, both of them found it difficult. "My wife called me five times a day saying, 'Where are you?' and we both felt disoriented and depressed for at least a month." His disorientation was compounded by the fact that people in the congregation were jealous of his time away, and resentful he had not been there when they felt they needed him. This made him reluctant to talk about his wonderful experiences when he returned.

A Catholic priest also spoke of disorientation—how the world of voice mail, keys, microphones at church, presiding at Mass all seemed strange after being away from them for so long.

A large number of clergy I interviewed had a more serious issue when they returned from sabbatical. They found a congregation or staff that had erupted in conflict, or was about to do so.

One pastor, though welcomed home warmly by the congregation, sensed immediately that something was wrong in the staff. A couple of staff members had complained about the pastor's management style to the fill-in pastors, who had taken the matter to the staff–parish committee in his absence. The result was hurt and confusion all around. It took a great deal of the pastor's emotional energy to deal with this conflict after his return.

University chaplain Linda Johnson was not prepared for her own resistance to returning to the rhythm of work. The adjustment from restfulness back to regimentation took her most of an academic semester.

Another pastor returned to a major church conflict. However, even while it was painful and difficult, she felt she and the church recovered from it quickly and were able to move on from it more easily than might have been the case a year earlier. She attributes this at least partly to her sabbatical and the new outlook it gave her.

On the other hand, there were clergy who found their reentry to be easy. For some the flurry of activity was a welcome change from the slower pace of leave-taking. They were welcomed back by healthy congregations who had missed them. They were eager to get back to work and found the transition from sabbatical to ministry a simple one.

Though planning does not ensure a conflict-free return or a simple transition from one mode to another, good planning and organization before and during the sabbatical can make reentry easier. Each congregation and staff should have a clear understanding of who will handle what responsibilities in the pastor's absence. Whether filled by paid staff or by volunteers, every duty needs to be assigned with clarity. In addition, if problems should arise, the congregation's leadership should know where to turn for help, rather than just wait for the pastor's return.

At the same time, clergy should anticipate needing time to catch up with what has been going on in the congregation during the sabbatical. Planning for this starts with deciding when to return. I can tell you from my experience that you should avoid high seasons or special times in the life of the congregation. It is much better to return during a "down time" than to enter caught up in the natural motion of all that accompanies those events. Prepare folks for the fact that you'd like to keep your first few weeks' schedule a little on the light side, so not everyone will want to make an appointment with you at once. Ease back into your responsibilities by asking some of the people who have taken on additional tasks to let go of them slowly. You might want some extra office help the first week or so, or someone to assist you with visiting. Perhaps your judicatory would excuse you from a meeting so you could have a night off with your family. Decide what are the most important tasks for you to tackle first, and do them. Leave some of the less important ones for the following month, or ask for assistance.

Finally, despite all that I've said, don't be afraid to return. Plan also to enjoy it. Though my first month back was tiring and chaotic, it was also delightful and fun. It was a great joy to see everyone again and to be welcomed back to the church. I loved sharing some of my sabbatical experiences with the congregation and hearing about theirs. The visual sermon I gave using slides of my photographs was a turning point in proving to myself that the sabbatical had really made a difference in me and my creativity. Most of all, the return to my work—my calling—was the culmination of all that had happened to me and in me.

For Inspiration

Make an entry in your journal about how it was the first week back at work. What were the events of the week? What were you feeling and thinking? Go back and read it a month or so later. What has changed?

Or, write about going to work after a long vacation.

For Contemplation

Read Psalm 100. What about your congregation and situation gives you cause for thanks? Can you remember what attracted you to these people in the first place?

For Action

1. Make a list of the things that have gone well since your return and the things that have not gone so well. Discuss the list (or various parts of it) with an appropriate group. For example, your Parish Relations Committee will want to know if there is conflict. Tell the governing board if you need more office help. Talk to the Education Committee to have someone take over the class you are teaching for a month until you can get your time back under control.
2. Plan several days off at the end of the first month or two. Spend those days in a relaxing setting and evaluate your work since your return from leave. What important learnings from your sabbatical do you feel may be slipping away? How can you recover them?

For Further Reading

Read chapter 11 (about "Homecoming") of Richard Bullock and Richard Bruesehoff's book *Clergy Renewal: The Alban Guide to Pastoral Sabbaticals* (Bethesda, Md.: The Alban Institute, 2000).

Chapter 12

You Did *What*?

Journal: Time to Reflect

January 28, 2002

Yesterday was our congregation's annual meeting. It is our time to review the year past and anticipate the year to come. According to our denomination, it is when we "... present the reports and recommendations of the organizations and groups in the particular church in a creative and innovative way that motivates members to mission."[1]

Among our various reports this year included a report from me about my clergy renewal leave. Even though there had been other opportunities for me to share some of my experiences, this was the time for a more formal report of what I had done and what I hoped the experience had accomplished for our congregation. More importantly, I set aside time for the congregation to talk about their experience of our time apart. I had talked with the session and other groups and individuals, but now I wanted an open, public discussion. More than two months have passed since my return, and I think enough time has gone by for us to have at least a little distance on the subject without the memory fading too much into the past.

Members made several comments that seemed to have a general consensus. First, the time I was away might have been more difficult if someone other than Florence had been the supply pastor. Florence meshed very well with our congregation. She has experience in and a particular affection for smaller churches. Her presence, both in and out of the pulpit, is quite genuine and pastoral. People expressed gratitude that she was available at least some of the time during the week for making pastoral calls and taking care of day-to-day issues. She worked well with our session and its committees. They seemed to think it was important to have the same person every week instead of a steady stream of supply preachers.

Second, our church office and all the important functions of the institution continued to hum along without any hitches. Largely, this was due to the coordination by Carol, our part-time secretary, and by the committees of the session. Nothing major went undone. Florence performed one wedding and two funerals. Enough people knew how to do enough things to perform all the necessary work of the church.

Third, people seemed surprised that everything went just fine. I think maybe they expected there to be a large gap in my absence, and it pleased us all when there was none. Attendance was normal; giving stayed current; new things happened. They were not just marking time or moving backwards. The study of spiritual gifts they undertook with Florence was not something I could have done well. With her different personality and strengths, they learned new things about themselves.

Fourth, many members seemed surprised to learn how much I do. Maybe this isn't such a bad thing. I took the opportunity to tell them I need to make my work hours more reasonable, and they were encouraging.

Finally, I took the opportunity once again to express my deep gratitude to the congregation for their support around my sabbatical. Knowing how capable they are, I had no worries about being away for several months. Trusting in their friendship, I had looked forward to my return. I listed my sabbatical accomplishments, emphasizing the things that had been most important to me: spiritual renewal; travel; time with Jerry; revitalization of my creativity through writing and photography. I assured them I had returned to them a rested and renewed pastor, ready to continue a long pastorate in their midst, listening with them for the next thing God was calling us to do together.

One fear I shared with those gathered yesterday was the fear of becoming stale. I have seen many churches and pastors get so comfortable with each other they seem to stop dreaming about the future. Ministries that were once innovative and vital outlived their usefulness, but either no one could see it or had the desire to do anything about it. After a number of years together, it can simply become easy to forget what we are about because the church is happy and the pastor is happy. I never want us to be so comfortable with each other that we forget what it is we are supposed to do.

With that in mind, I told the congregation yesterday that I hoped this time of renewal would do just that: Renew us in our love for God and each other, and renew us in our mission together. I want to stay here. And I want to keep listening.

Evaluating Together

After you have had time to settle back into a routine of sorts, it is time for you and the congregation to evaluate just what did take place, and how it affected all of you. Too often, clergy forget this important step in the sabbatical process. If part of the purpose of clergy renewal is time for reflection, then now is the time to look back and reflect together. Your congregation and you have invested significant amounts of time, energy, and money in the sabbatical. Just giving a slide show of your travels or thanking them for the time off is not enough. They deserve the opportunity to reflect together about what happened, to think about what went well and what didn't go well, and to give thanks. This process also begins to lay the ground for the next sabbatical a few years down the road.

This evaluation can take any number of forms. Depending on the size and style of the congregation, you might work more or less formally. The more settings in which evaluation can happen, the more accurate picture you will have.

An evaluation is the opportunity for reflection on a corporate scale. During your sabbatical, you have time to reflect on your calling as it relates to your current setting. Now it is the congregation's turn. You can help them think beyond "extended vacation for the pastor" and "let us just get through this sabbatical until things can get back to normal," to what they have experienced and learned. They can also see how they can benefit from your sabbatical experience.

If conflict has occurred while you were away or since you returned, the corporate reflection takes on even more importance. Let the congregation examine the roots of the conflict and how it can be managed or directed. Sometimes an outsider can help with this process, particularly if the conflict involves you. A trusted colleague trained in conflict management, a judicatory official with the appropriate skills, or even a consultant may be the right person to assist the congregation through this process. Don't feel as though you have to walk through the conflict alone. This is always true. We may think we need to handle things by ourselves, but that's usually the wrong approach. Even when there is no major conflict, it may still be helpful to work through the evaluative process with outside assistance.

Keep in mind also that new conflict may emerge during the evaluation process. This is another excellent reason to have a facilitator there. Perhaps some parishioner will come forward with resentment over your having been away or having missed an important event (a funeral, perhaps). Someone may use the evaluation as an excuse to raise previously unmentioned issues about your ministry. These possibilities are always present during assessments, but a sabbatical may give ammunition to someone who is looking for it.

There are several good books available to help with evaluating congregations and clergy (see references at the end of this chapter). Some of their forms and ideas can easily be adapted to the purpose of evaluating the sabbatical experience. Both you and the congregation should make the time to share the positive and negative aspects of your renewal leave, and imagine how both clergy and organization might learn and change from it.

Informal processes work well, too. Each committee or work group can take some time at a meeting a few months after the sabbatical to discuss its effects. Did the youth group continue to meet regularly, and did the young people bond with different adults? How was the annual stewardship campaign affected by the pastor's absence? What was it like for the choir and other musicians if they had to adapt to a different worship leader each week? How did they decide who would choose the music? Did the office staff find it difficult to function without the regular presence of a full-time pastor? Was the professional staff comfortable taking on new responsibilities? How did the Bible study group like a different style of teaching? Were any big projects put on hold during the pastor's absence? Perhaps most importantly, was the congregation's mission advanced during this time, or did it stand still or even take a step backwards?

A significant group to work with in this process is the parish relations or personnel committee. If there were conflicts or problems, the members of this committee should be aware of them. Since they were involved in the planning of the sabbatical, they will be very attentive to its results. Therefore, the pastor will be particularly interested in this group's insights and opinions.

Of course, the governing board will have opinions about what has transpired. Allow a good portion of one of their meetings to let them talk about their experience and to share yours with them.

It is also important at some point to let the whole congregation hear a report from you and have the chance to talk. Our annual meeting came at just the right time; you may have to schedule a congregational forum for just that purpose. A church dinner is perfect for this type of discussion. One idea is to have a list of questions for "table talk," and put a member of your governing board or parish relations committee at each table. During the meal they can ask: What was the best part of the sabbatical time from your perspective? What was difficult? What kind of growth has our congregation experienced as a result? What should we do differently the next time?

Have someone from each table give a brief report of their discussion. List the items in a visible way. This is a great time for you to talk about your time away, using slides of your travels, showing what you accomplished, trying to convey just how it felt to have the time for other pursuits. Allow people to celebrate with you, enjoying vicariously the fruits of your time away.

An additional purpose of this public meeting may be to dream together about the future. This is a great time to begin imagining together new directions and new mission. As your governing board or parish relations committee hears these discussions, they can go back and begin working through the next steps of planning and implementation.

It is your privilege to guide and lead in these next steps. Now is the time to begin bringing forward all those exciting thoughts and plans you had during your months away. What were the ideas that stirred your faithful imagination? Which undertakings now seem most suited for this time and place? Share your proposals with the governing board. They will likely be open to new projects in the post-sabbatical time, which already has a transitional feel to it. In some ways, you are once again like the new pastor in this setting, except now you have the trust and friendship of the congregation and board, which you have earned over the years.

Is your congregation ready to think about a significant new mission outreach? Is it time to consider redevelopment? Perhaps you want to consider making significant changes in your worship services, or start a building project. Maybe you have seen something important you never noticed before because you were too close, but when you stepped back it was clear as could be. How has your consciousness of the current situation been raised by your new experiences?

Take the time carefully to explain and show to the appropriate groups in your congregation the changes in your outlook. Give them room to express their reactions and to enlarge upon or take issue with your ideas. Using your skills to work through change, begin to move with the leadership and the rest of the congregation toward finding that new place to which you are all being called.

For Inspiration

Write in your journal about your hopes and dreams for the future of your congregation. You have been there long enough to earn a sabbatical. Now what do you imagine for the years between now and the next sabbatical?

For Contemplation

How will the process of evaluation help your congregation see its purpose in new ways?

For Action

Plan an evaluation process. It may be helpful to use some of the good evaluation materials that are on the market. Perhaps the evaluation of the sabbatical experience can coincide with the annual evaluation of program and staff. Decide who should be included and who will facilitate.

For Further Study

Hudson, Jill M. *Evaluating Ministry: Principles and Processes for Clergy and Congregations.* Washington, D.C.: The Alban Institute, 1992.

Woods, C. Jeff. *User-Friendly Evaluation: Improving the Work of Pastors, Programs, and Laity.* Washington, D.C.: The Alban Institute, 1995.

Chapter 13

The New Pastor

Journal: The Recliner

May 17, 2002

It has been more than nine months since I began my sabbatical, and about six months since I completed it. Though it will be another year, at least, before I can take a long-enough view back to have a fuller perspective on what has changed, I can already see change in some very important areas.

The most important new symbol in my life is a reclining chair. On my first day back to work in November, I walked by an adult classroom and saw three new upholstered chairs in a corner. I strolled over to examine them. Two were recliners and one was a swivel rocker. I surmised someone had donated them to the church. Later, back in my office, I couldn't get those chairs out of my mind. Hadn't I been thinking about needing new chairs in my office? The current ones were covered in orange vinyl, and one was broken. The chairs in the classroom happened to match my office décor better than they did that of the classroom, and didn't that class always sit around the tables, anyway?

Alone in the building that November day, I spent a good 45 minutes maneuvering the platform rocker and one of the recliners down the hall, up a long flight of narrow stairs (the recliner had to be smushed through the doorway to the stairwell) and down the other hall to my office. There they were traded for the orange vinyl ones, and there they have remained. I learned later that week the source of the chairs, and received enthusiastic permission to put them in my office where I promised they would be both used and appreciated. And they have been.

For some reason, it became extremely important to my just-back-to-work psyche to get that recliner in my office before the end of that first day. I couldn't wait until the next day when the secretary would be there and could help me move them. Not a single office day has passed since then when I have not spent a few minutes sitting in that chair. It has become my symbol of the new me.

The recliner is now the place where I spend my devotional time. It helps me to come out from behind my desk where, when I read the scriptures, it is usually for preparing a sermon or a Bible study lesson. Instead, I sit in an easy chair, and I read the Bible for more personal reasons, and even for fun. Prayer in the recliner is, for some reason, less structured and more honest than it is at the desk. Sometimes I eat lunch in the recliner, or read the mail. It has become an oasis in my office. I can take a mini-vacation from work and stress just by walking across the room, sitting down, and putting up my feet. The presence of the recliner reminds me of what I should do often, of what I promised myself.

I can read back over my journal entries from the last several years, and easily see where change was needed. Now I am glad to say that much of what I needed to do personally has been accomplished. Not that things are now perfectly balanced and in order, but the difference is evident.

My work hours are now much more under control than they have been in 10 years. I knew from the beginning this would be the most important and difficult hurdle for me, and that has proved true. After a pressured first month back from sabbatical, I took a good hard look at where I was and where I wanted to be. Something had to give, and I began then making choices about hours at work. Otherwise, I knew I'd end up right back where I started. In the last several months, those choices have become easier with practice. I have learned how to say "no" more easily. Jerry and I have enjoyed more time together as a direct result.

In deciding how better to use my time, my spiritual life is now a higher priority. I was not willing to give up the gains I made during the sabbatical, and I have renewed my commitment to spend more time in prayer and Bible study. I doubt if this has paid off in any visible or even concrete ways, but I do believe that at some level it is continuing to make me into a better pastor. Communing with God makes me more able to help others do the same.

My desire and ability to plan for the church has grown immensely in the past few months. I believe this is a direct result of working fewer hours and having a more rested mind. In April I attended a conference on the subject of transformational ministry and have begun working with the session on redevelopment issues for our congregation. We are not a prime placement for redevelopment, but our community is changing and our church needs to decide what we will do in response to those changes. The session has given me an enthusiastic go-ahead to form an idea-generating planning group that will look as objectively as possible at our changing community, and look ahead at where we want the church to go. Since we have recently celebrated 10 years together, now is an appropriate time for some sort of evaluation of where we have come from, where we are, and where we are going. We have so much to celebrate about what we've accomplished in the last several years. At the same time, we need to continue to look ahead. Our planning group will work alongside the current system, thinking as creatively as possible about what God may be calling us to do.

My newfound creativity has not been confined to my work. It has continued to be a part of my personal life. Last month Jerry and I spent 10 days in New Mexico, a place neither of us had visited. Mostly, we hiked and took pictures. We spent long minutes deciding how to frame and meter particular settings, and we came home with some great photographs. On several other occasions I have just taken the camera and gone out to photograph our garden plants with a macro lens, or the church steeple on a clear day. I've also been setting aside time for more writing and have found it to be both relaxing and productive. Sometimes my best ideas for church come to me when I am writing about something else entirely.

Sabbath has found a new place in my life. All tied up with creativity, fewer work hours, and a deepening spiritual life is the understanding that sabbath is essential to my well-being. Though I don't always succeed, I try to make a day each week where I am doing the things that bring me closer to God. These days usually involve gardening, baking bread, resting, taking pictures, spending time with Jerry, or some combination.

Time is the central theme in all these changes I've made. By rethinking my use of time, I have been able to achieve a new balance among the various parts of me. No longer do I feel so weighed down by just a few things. I do have a sense of feeling lighter, more responsive to new congregational needs as they arise, more able to lead the church into our next phase of living together as God's people.

What Has Changed?

Over the last few decades many have written about the need for leading congregations through the difficulties inherent in change. We have focused less on the need for change within the very pastors who lead those congregations. I believe it sometimes takes an outside force or event—something out of the ordinary—to help a pastor realize change is necessary and possible. For some, that event has been a sabbatical experience. Dave Holte says this in reflecting on his clergy renewal leave:

> I am quite different now. I realize that my life is more important than any one congregation, that the world is bigger than Brainerd, Minnesota, and that life is too short to waste it on work all the time. I have lowered my expectations of myself, and I think I am more realistic about having to prove myself all the time. Parish ministry is pretty much impossible, so to maintain a healthy life, you have to be realistic. Sabbatical helped me realize that there is a whole big world out there and I can do something else if I so choose. I think I am a better pastor now, too, by living like "them" for three months. Everyone has challenges in life—even those who don't work on weekends!

When asked how he changed as a result of his sabbatical, Steven Reuben says, "I'm not sure, except I take care of myself better. I feel a greater sense of personal space and distance with the congregation and not so much enmeshed in everything even though I am still passionate about my work and life." This is not a small thing. As we've said throughout this book, a pastoral leader who is stressed is less effective. One who is well rested and has a strong sense of self is much better able to lead others.

This strong sense of self-differentiation is extremely important. Sometimes we have to be away from our work for a while to realize deep within ourselves that we are not what we do. Perhaps this is more true of long-term pastorates, when the lives of pastor and congregation understandably become more intertwined over time. A period of reconnecting with oneself helps the pastor to gain distance on the congregational relationship. Physical distance can encourage a healthy emotional distance. Listen to Arthur Boers: "I remember, when I traveled to Europe, that one day I was thinking about problems in the church that had not been resolved before I left. I consciously noted that that was all 'so far away' and was then able to let it go. That was a great thing for a worrier like me."

Letting go of things is a great way to get to a healthier place for both clergy and congregation. It's almost as though we make room in our minds and hearts for more creative thinking when we clean out the space we use for worry, anxiety, and all those other destructive, time-consuming thoughts and emotions. Letting go is disconnecting. Disconnecting any unhealthy circuits between pastor and congregation allows for reconnecting in healthier ways. In some cases, seeing conflicts elsewhere brought a better understanding to situations at home. "Spending time in Northern Ireland and the Middle East also gave me new perspective on the spiritual strains of dealing with conflict in the local parish," says Bill Schooler.

Surprisingly few pastors told me the sabbatical had made them ready to leave their congregations. Instead, several who had originally thought they might leave decided to stay. It seems that the time away, of disconnecting, made them more able to stay for the long haul. The distance brought them a different view. Jill Hudson, a Presbyterian judicatory official, notes that long-term pastors return from sabbaticals "refreshed and energized for the next round of service. If they wait too long for the sabbatical they sometimes come back and leave because they realize they cannot re-up in this setting."

Many clergy who have spouses and/or children found the sabbatical to be a time of rediscovering the importance of those relationships. It is not a new thought that many of us tend to put our families second to our work, especially when the work is "God's work." Over time, particularly in long-term pastorates, family and other important relationships can slip further and further down our unwritten list of priorities. Once the habit becomes ingrained, it gets easier to miss a ballgame or to attend one more important committee meeting instead of having an evening at home. Family members, too, get used to the pastor being gone more and more. Little wonder the divorce rate is high among clergy.

Sabbatical, like the sabbath, breaks into the streams of our habits and makes us take a look at how we have been living. It exposes the mistakes we make in our prioritizing, because sabbath is about time. It holds up as an example a different way of living. So many clergy, after having enjoyed this new space with their families, realize they cannot go back to the old ways of always putting work first. Holly McKissick, for example, realized when she spent major hunks of time with her daughter and son (aged six and three) in France and Italy that they finally "broke with habits of not connecting," habits they'd formed over the years of her ministry. Now she is consciously putting more things aside in order to spend time with them, and she is learning how to draw better boundaries with the congregation in order to have a fuller family life.

In a final word, I discovered in my own experience, and in the experiences of those I interviewed, that sabbaticals are important instruments for change in the lives of both congregation and clergy. They may be an untapped resource as we look to the future of churches in a changing society. What would be the result if every clergyperson, after five or six years with a congregation, had the opportunity to step back and take a new look at the situation? What would happen if every congregation used the time to rethink a part of its mission and ministry, preparing for a period of conscious refocusing after the pastor's return? What would happen if the pastor could spend the time renewing his heart for and call to that particular congregation, and reconnecting with her faith, herself, and her close relationships? What more could we accomplish as God's people if we took the sabbath time to listen for God's voice, and set up the mechanisms to allow ourselves and our congregations the freedom to then act upon that voice?

Like your story, mine is not yet over. How this sabbatical will continue to affect me and this congregation is an ending waiting to be written. I will keep writing about it in my journal, keep looking for ways to live it. The joy of seeking and finding sabbath, and the joy of letting sabbath change us, never ends.

Notes

Chapter One

1. Roy M. Oswald, *Clergy Self-Care: Finding a Balance for Effective Ministry* (Washington, D.C.: The Alban Institute, 1991).

2. Presbyterian Church (USA), "The Presbyterian Panel Report: Background Report for the 1997–1999 Presbyterian Panel" (Louisville: Research Services, Presbyterian Church (USA), 2000).

3. Glenn E. Ludwig, *In It for the Long Haul: Building Effective Long-Term Pastorates* (Bethesda, Md.: The Alban Institute, 2002).

4. James P. Wind and Gilbert R. Rendle, *The Leadership Situation Facing American Congregations: An Alban Institute Special Report* (Bethesda, Md.: The Alban Institute, 2001). Available online at www.alban.org/leadership.asp.

5. Henri J. M. Nouwen, *Sabbatical Journey: The Diary of His Final Year* (New York: Crossroad, 1998).

Chapter Two

1. Richard J. Bruesehoff is co-author, with A. Richard Bullock, of *Clergy Renewal: The Alban Guide to Sabbatical Planning* (Bethesda, Md.: The Alban Institute, 2000).

Chapter Three

1. Roy M. Oswald, *Why You Should Give Your Pastor a Sabbatical* (video) (Bethesda, Md.: The Alban Institute, 2001).

2. A. Richard Bullock and Richard J. Bruesehoff, *Clergy Renewal: The Alban Guide to Sabbatical Planning* (Bethesda, Md.: The Alban Institute, 2000).

Chapter Nine

1. Marva J. Dawn, *Keeping the Sabbath Wholly: Ceasing, Resting, Embracing, Feasting* (Grand Rapids, Mich.: Wm. B. Eerdmans, 1999), 5.
2. Wayne Muller, *Sabbath: Finding Rest, Renewal, and Delight in Our Busy Lives* (New York: Bantam Books, 2000), 101.
3. Dawn, *Keeping the Sabbath Wholly*, 53.

Chapter Twelve

1. *The Constitution of the Presbyterian Church (USA), Part II, Book of Order 2001–2002* (Louisville: The Office of the General Assembly, Presbyterian Church [USA], 2001), G-7.0302.

Welcome to the work of Alban Institute...
the leading publisher and congregational
resource organization for clergy and laity today.

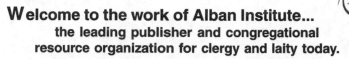

Your purchase of this book means you have an interest in the kinds of information, research, consulting, networking opportunities and educational seminars that Alban Institute produces and provides. We are a non-denominational, non-profit 25-year-old membership organization dedicated to providing practical and useful support to religious congregations and those who participate in and lead them.

Alban is acknowledged as a pioneer in learning and teaching on *Conflict Management *Faith and Money *Congregational Growth and Change *Leadership Development *Mission and Planning *Clergy Recruitment and Training *Clergy Support, Self-Care and Transition *Spirituality and Faith Development *Congregational Security.

Our membership is comprised of over 8,000 clergy, lay leaders, congregations and institutions who benefit from:
❖ 15% discount on hundreds of Alban books
❖ $50 per-course tuition discount on education seminars
❖ Subscription to *Congregations*, the Alban journal (a $30 value)
❖ Access to Alban research and (soon) the "Members-Only" archival section of our web site www.alban.org

For more information on Alban membership or to be added to our catalog mailing list, call 1-800-486-1318, ext.243 or return this form.

Name and Title: _____

Congregation/Organization: _____

Address: _____

City: _____ Tel.: _____

State: _____ Zip: _____ Email: _____

BKIN

The Alban Institute
Attn: Membership Dept.
7315 Wisconsin Avenue
Suite 1250 West
Bethesda, MD 20814-3211